THE WORLD OF MYTHOLOGY

MESOAMERICAN MYTH

A TREASURY OF CENTRAL AMERICAN LEGENDS, ART, AND HISTORY

First published in North America in 2008 by M.E. Sharpe, Inc.

Sharpe Focus
An imprint of M.E. Sharpe, Inc.
80 Business Park Drive
Armonk, NY 10504
www.mesharpe.com

Copyright © 2008 Marshall Editions
A Marshall Edition
Conceived, edited, and designed by Marshall Editions
The Old Brewery, 6 Blundell Street, London N7 9BH, U.K.
www.quarto.com

Library of Congress Cataloging-in-Publication Data

Ganeri, Anita, 1961-
  Mesoamerican myth : a treasury of Central American legends, art, and
history / Anita Ganeri.
     p. cm. -- (The world of mythology)
  Includes bibliographical references and index.
  ISBN 978-0-7656-8106-5 (hardcover : alk. paper)
  1. Aztec mythology--Juvenile literature. 2. Maya mythology--Juvenile
literature. I. Title.

F1219.76.R45G36 2008
299.7'842013--dc22
                                            2007005877

Originated in Hong Kong by Modern Age
Printed and bound in China by Midas Printing Limited

10 9 8 7 6 5 4 3 2 1

Publisher: Richard Green
Commissioning editor: Claudia Martin
Art direction: Ivo Marloh
Picture manager: Veneta Bullen
Design and editorial: Tall Tree Ltd.
Production: Nikki Ingram

Previous page: This step pyramid stands in the ceremonial center of Tikal in present-day Guatemala.
This page and opposite: The ruins of ancient temples rise out of the jungle at Tikal. The city was a major cultural center of Maya civilization. It reached its height during the Maya Classic Period, about 250–900 C.E., but was abandoned by the end of the tenth century.

THE WORLD OF MYTHOLOGY

MESOAMERICAN MYTH

A TREASURY OF CENTRAL AMERICAN LEGENDS, ART, AND HISTORY

ANITA GANERI

Sharpe Focus
an imprint of M.E. Sharpe, Inc.

CONTENTS

AZTEC CREATION MYTHS

TALES OF THE AZTEC GODS

MAYA CREATION MYTHS

TALES OF THE HERO TWINS

INTRODUCTION

When Spanish explorers reached the region known today as
Mesoamerica in the sixteenth century, they encountered two
highly sophisticated civilizations—the Aztecs and the Maya.
Both lived in great cities with complex forms of government and
administration. Both had highly developed calendars and systems
of writing. And both had rich collections of myths through which
they sought to understand the natural world, which they believed
was created and controlled by a wide range of deities.

The Aztecs were a Mesoamerican people of central Mexico who conquered an extensive empire during the fourteenth, fifteenth, and sixteenth centuries. In the mid-1300s, they settled in the Valley of Mexico, where they founded the great city of Tenochtitlan (teh-noch-TEE-tlahn) on a group of islands in Lake Texcoco (tesh-KOH-koh). The city quickly grew in size and importance and became the capital of the mighty Aztec Empire. From this base, the Aztecs conquered many other peoples in central and southern Mexico and demanded tribute from them in the form of crops and goods. The empire reached the height of its powers in the early 1500s but was destroyed in 1521 by Spanish invaders, led by Hernando Cortés (1485–1547). Greedy for Aztec gold, the Spanish killed the Aztec emperor and reduced Tenochtitlan to ruins.

WHO WERE THE MAYA?

Maya civilization emerged as early as 1000 B.C.E and gradually spread throughout the eastern part of Mesoamerica. It reached its peak in the so-called Classic Period, about 250–900 C.E. Although the Maya shared one language, culture, and religion, they did not have a united government or capital city. Each of their great cities, such as Tikal and Chichen Itza, had its own ruler. During the eighth and ninth centuries, Maya culture went into decline and many cities in the central lowlands were abandoned.

Several factors may have caused this, including drought, overcrowding, and disease. But the Maya continued to survive in Yucatan (in present-day Mexico) and the Guatemalan highlands. From the 1520s, Spanish invaders began to take control of the Maya lands, although the last Maya state was not conquered until 1697.

AZTEC AND MAYA MYTHS

Since language emerged, people in every world culture have told traditional stories to explain particular beliefs, customs and rituals, or mysterious natural phenomena. These stories are called myths. Both the Aztecs and Maya had rich and complex collections of myths. Contact between the two cultures through migration, trade, and conquest led to many mythological themes being shared. The Mesoamerican myths are fascinating not just for the stories they tell but also for what they reveal about Aztec and Maya life, beliefs, and culture.

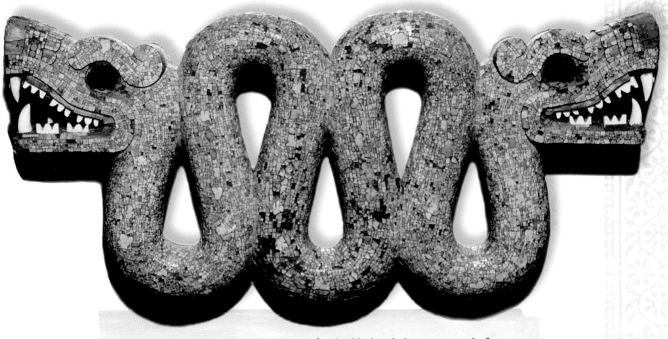

Above: This ornament in the shape of a double-headed serpent, made from wood, shell, and precious jade, dates from the fifteenth century. A symbol of Tlaloc (TLAH-lock), the Aztec god of rain and fertility, it was worn by a high priest. It may have formed part of the treasure sent by the Aztec emperor Moctezuma II to the Spanish conquerors.

In both cultures, important myths were told about how the world was created, and is sustained, by the gods, with whom both peoples had an intense relationship. Myths also shed light on Aztec and Maya beliefs about the human condition: how and why people were created, why they are flawed, why they must eventually die, and what happens to them after death. Natural phenomena, such as the rising of the Sun in the sky, were similarly explained. Additionally, in Aztec mythology, the origins and growth of the Aztec Empire were reflected in their stories, such as the migration of the Aztecs from Aztlan, and the birth of Huitzilopochtli (weet-sill-oh-POSH-tlee), the Aztecs' patron god.

To the Aztecs and Maya, their myths were viewed as part of their history, although scholars treat the relationship between history and myth-making with caution. Some episodes, such as the story of the migration of the Aztecs, may well have been based in fact, and some of the places mentioned, such as the cities of Tollan and Tenochtitlan, are known to have existed from archaeological evidence. In many accounts, however, myth and history are so densely blended that facts are hard to identify and interpret.

Myths also contained lessons about the correct way to behave. In the Aztec story of "The Rabbit and the Moon," for example, it is not the vain and proud god, Tecuciztecatl (the-kuh-sis-TAY-cahtl), who becomes the all-important Sun, but the modest and brave Nanahuatzin (nah-nah-WHAT-sin). In the Maya myths of the Hero Twins, the twins kill the monstrous bird, Seven Macaw, because of his misplaced arrogance and boasting.

SOURCES OF MYTHS

At first, both Aztec and Maya myths were passed on by word of mouth. Later, both of these cultures developed highly sophisticated systems of writing, and recorded their myths in words and pictures in codices (hand-written books), in carved inscriptions on stone slabs called stelae, and on painted vases. Unfortunately, much of this material was destroyed by the Spanish invaders. The most important sources that exist for Aztec mythology come from the period after the Spanish conquest. These were written by Aztecs who learned Spanish and by Spanish monks who studied Aztec language and culture. The most important Maya sources were written by the Maya themselves. Of these, the outstanding document is the *Popol Vuh* (poh-pol voo), or "Book of the Community," of the Quiche Maya of Guatemala. Divided into sections, it begins with the Maya creation myth, followed by the exploits of the mythical Hero Twins.

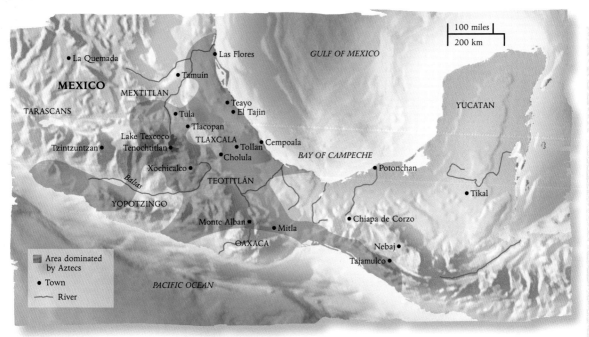

MEXICO
TARASCANS
MEXTITLAN
La Quemada •
• Tamuín
• Las Flores
• Teayo
• Tula   • El Tajin
• Tlacopan
Lake Texcoco
Tzintzuntzan •   Tenochtitlan •   TLAXCALA
• Tollan   • Cempoala
• Xochicalco   • Cholula
Balsas
TEOTITLÁN
YOPOTZINGO
Monte Alban •   • Mitla
OAXACA
• Chiapa de Corzo
Nebaj •
Tajamulco •

GULF OF MEXICO

YUCATAN

BAY OF CAMPECHE

• Potonchan

• Tikal

100 miles
200 km

Area dominated by Aztecs
• Town
— River

PACIFIC OCEAN

Above: This map shows, in orange, the area dominated by the Aztecs at the height of their power and influence in 1520 C.E. The Aztec Empire was centered on the great city of Tenochtitlan.

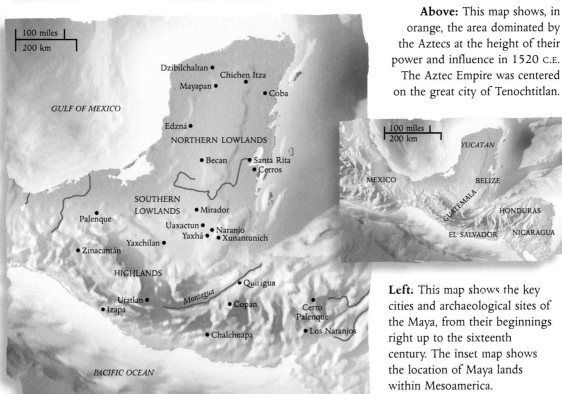

100 miles
200 km

GULF OF MEXICO

Dzibilchaltan •   • Chichen Itza
Mayapan •   • Coba

Edzná •
NORTHERN LOWLANDS

• Becan   • Santa Rita
• Cerros

SOUTHERN
LOWLANDS   • Mirador
Palenque •   Uaxactun •   • Naranjo
Yaxchilan •   Yaxhá •   • Xunantunich
• Zinacantán

HIGHLANDS
Quirigua •
Utatlan •   Montagua   • Copan
• Izapa   Cerro Palenque
• Los Naranjos
• Chalchuapa

PACIFIC OCEAN

100 miles
200 km

YUCATAN

MEXICO   BELIZE

GUATEMALA   HONDURAS

EL SALVADOR   NICARAGUA

Left: This map shows the key cities and archaeological sites of the Maya, from their beginnings right up to the sixteenth century. The inset map shows the location of Maya lands within Mesoamerica.

Introduction   9

The ruins of the Pyramid of the Sun at the ancient city of Teotihuacan still stand about 25 miles (40 km) to the northeast of Mexico City. The Aztecs believed that this was where the gods gathered at the end of the Fourth Sun to decide who would become the new, Fifth Sun.

AZTEC CREATION MYTHS

The Aztecs had many myths about how the Earth was created. They did not believe that the world they lived in was the first to have ever existed. Rather, they believed that there had been four previous creations, called the four "Suns." Each of these had ended in disaster before the next came into being. The current age was known as the "Fifth Sun."

The Aztecs believed that, one day, this world too would end catastrophically, possibly destroyed by a gigantic earthquake. Because of this belief, they lived in constant fear, never knowing when their world was about to end. Each day, they watched anxiously for the Sun to rise in the sky, marking the beginning of a new day. They also offered daily sacrifices to keep the gods happy. They hoped that this would keep the Sun alive and postpone their ultimate destruction.

THE FOUR PAST WORLDS

Four gods ruled over the four past worlds. God of the night, Tezcatlipoca (tes-kah-tlee-POH-ka), presided over the First Sun. God of the wind, Quetzalcoatl (ket-sahl-KOH-ahtl), ruled over the Second Sun. The Third Sun was created by the rain god, Tlaloc (TLAH-lock), while his wife, Chalchiuhtlicue (chahl-chee-oo-TLEE-kway), goddess of oceans and rivers, created the Fourth Sun. But each of these bright new Suns was doomed to meet a disastrous end.

When the world was bathed in darkness, in the long days before the First Sun began, the great creator, Ometeotl (oh-may-TAY-ohtl), lived in the thirteenth and highest level of heaven. Ometeotl had four sons, called the four Tezcatlipocas, to whom he gave the mighty task of creating the gods and goddesses, the world, and human beings to live in it. For six hundred years, the Tezcatlipocas delayed. Then, at last, two of them began the work of creation. First, they created fire. Then they made the Earth from a crocodile. They fixed the dates of the sacred calendar and forged the great, gloomy underworld of Mictlan (MEEK-tlahn).

THE JAGUAR SUN

When this was done, the god of the night, Black Tezcatlipoca, rose into the sky and transformed himself into the Sun. And so the first creation began. At that time, there were no human beings on Earth. The land was filled with towering giants who were so strong that they could rip up the trees from the rocky mountainsides and hurl them through the air. However, despite their size, the giants were not bloodthirsty creatures. They lived harmlessly on a diet of acorns, berries, and roots.

Black Tezcatlipoca's rule lasted for 676 years. Then his brother, White Tezcatlipoca, better known as Quetzalcoatl, grew tired of seeing his brother ruling over the world. Using a giant staff, he knocked his rival clean out of the sky and into the deep, dark sea.

THE AZTEC CALENDAR

The Aztecs were fascinated by the passage of time. They had two calendars: a solar calendar and a sacred calendar. The solar calendar was 365 days long and consisted of eighteen months of twenty days each, plus five extra days. The sacred calendar had 260 days. It was used by Aztec priests to determine auspicious days for activities, such as sowing crops and going to war. A combination of the two calendars led to cycles of fifty-two years. The end of a cycle was a particularly anxious time and was marked by an important ritual during which the Aztecs let their home fires go out. Only when, and if, the new year started, could a new fire be lit. Unless this happened, the terrifying demons of darkness might take control of the world.

Right: This enormous Aztec sculpture is known as the "Calendar Stone." At the center is the face of the Sun, surrounded by the twenty days of the solar calendar month. The symbols represent the Aztec belief in the past Four Suns and in the Fifth Sun, which will be destroyed by earthquakes.

With no Sun to light the sky, the Earth was plunged into darkness. But Black Tezcatlipoca, now known simply as Tezcatlipoca, was not finished yet. In his fury, he burst up out of the water in the shape of a ferocious jaguar.

Howling in anger, Tezcatlipoca raced across the plains and mountains, summoning jaguars wherever he went. The jaguars hunted down the giants and killed every single one of them. Then, still in his jaguar form, Tezcatlipoca leaped back into the sky, where he can still be seen today in the constellation that we know as the Great Bear.

SUNS OF WIND AND RAIN

Quetzalcoatl, god of the wind, took over the heavens in his brother's place. And so the second creation, the Sun of the Wind, began. Quetzalcoatl set a second Sun in the sky, and light returned to the dark world. His rule lasted for 364 years. During this time, the people of Earth looked more like human beings and lived on the seeds of the mesquite (mess-KEET) tree.

But this newfound peace did not last for long, for Tezcatlipoca was determined to take his terrible revenge. For years, he had plotted how to bring the Sun of the Wind to an end.

To overwhelm the wind god, Tezcatlipoca summoned a mighty, swirling hurricane which swept the Sun from the sky and the people from the Earth. When, finally, the storm subsided, everything was silent and still. Again darkness covered the world. Only a few creatures survived the storm, by clambering up into the few trees that were still left standing. There were no longer any people: they had all turned into monkeys in the trees, chattering and squawking in the deepening gloom.

When the Sun of the Wind ended, the great god of rain, Tlaloc, rose into the sky and took charge. And so the third creation, the Sun of the Rain, began. It was during this time, some legends say, that human beings once more appeared on Earth. They discovered the skills of farming and began to cultivate maize and other crops. But like the two Suns before it, the Sun of the Rain was doomed.

Once again, mighty Quetzalcoatl was the destroyer. After 312 years of Tlaloc's rule, Quetzalcoatl summoned a violent volcano which poured a blazing rain of fire and flames over the Earth. In the space of a day, the Sun was driven from the sky, and the handful of humans that were left alive after the burning were turned into turkeys, dogs, and butterflies.

THE WATER SUN

After the Sun of the Rain had ended, Tlaloc's wife, Chalchiuhtlicue, the goddess of lakes, oceans, and rivers, became the Sun. So the fourth creation began, and again human beings walked the Earth. Chalchiuhtlicue's rule lasted for 676 years, as long as the two previous creations combined. This time, it was the goddess herself who brought her own Sun to an end by sending a gigantic flood to cover the land and drown all living things.

One human couple, called Nata (NAH-tah) and Nena (NAY-nah), were warned about the flood by the god Tezcatlipoca.

"Stop whatever it is you are doing," he ordered, "and build a boat as fast as you can. For provisions, you should take just one ear of corn each to eat."

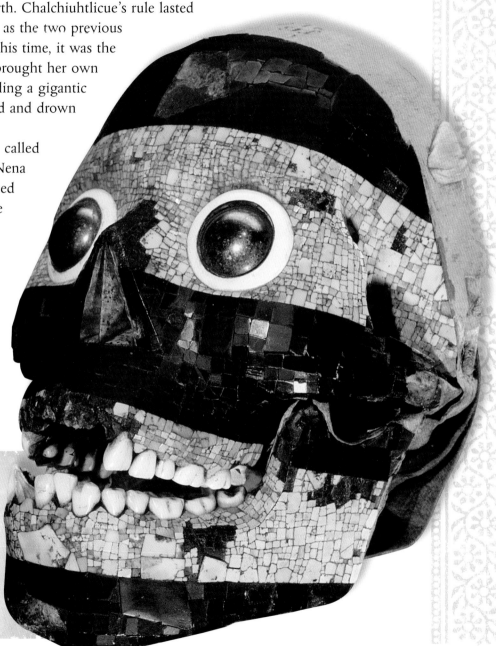

Right: This mask of the god Tezcatlipoca was made from shell, turquoise, lignite (coal), and a human skull. Tezcatlipoca was god of the night and of the north, and Quetzalcoatl's arch rival.

THE AZTEC UNIVERSE

The Aztecs believed that the Earth was shaped like a large disc, surrounded by water. From its center, the Earth spread out in the four points of the compass. Each of these directions was linked to one of the creator gods of the Four Suns (north: Tezcatlipoca; west: Quetzalcoatl; south: Tlaloc; east: Chalchiuhtlicue). The Fifth Sun was linked to the center, under the control of Xiuhtechuhtli (shoo tay-COO-tlee), the fire god. Above the Earth rose thirteen levels of heaven. Ometeotl, the supreme creator, lived in the highest two levels. Below the Earth were nine levels of Mictlan, the underworld.

Below: This illustration comes from the Codex Fejervary-Mayer. It shows the fire god Xiuhtechuhtli at the center of the universe.

Without thinking twice, Nata and Nena did what they were told. They cut down a towering cypress tree and hollowed out its trunk to make a boat. On board, they built a small cabin in which to shelter from the rain. They were just in time. No sooner had they finished than the waters came crashing down. The flood lasted for fifty-two years and was so terrible that it even washed the mighty mountains away.

Safe from the flood in their little boat, Nata and Nena were the only people to escape. But their ears of corn did not last long and soon they were hungry again.

"Oh, where on Earth will we find food?" said Nata. "There's nothing but water for miles around."

But when they clambered on top of their cabin to look, they saw that the water was teeming with life. For the human beings that Nata and Nena had left behind had been turned into fish!

"We need never go hungry again!" they cried.

Nata fashioned a fishing rod out of some sticks, while Nena made a fire. Soon smoke from the fire was rising into the sky and four large fish were roasting on it. Nata and Nena ate up the fish ravenously—and it tasted like the best meal that they had ever had.

However, the couple were so busy eating that they did not notice how the smoke from their fire was rising up into the sky and through the thirteen levels of heaven. There the smell angered some of the gods, who complained bitterly to Tezcatlipoca. Furious, Tezcatlipoca confronted Nata and Nena. He told them that they must be punished for disobeying his command and eating more than their one ear of corn—and straight away turned them into dogs. And so the fourth creation, the Water Sun, came to an end.

A NEW EARTH AND SKY

When, after many long years, the floodwaters finally subsided, the Earth lay in ruins. It was left to the quarrelsome gods Tezcatlipoca and Quetzalcoatl to set aside their differences and create a new world. On their travels, they met the great earth monster Tlaltecuhtli (tlal-the-KOO-tlee), swimming in the waters left by the flood. The gods immediately pounced on Tlaltecuhtli, killed her, and threw her tail into the sky to make the heavens. Then they fashioned the Earth from her head. Trees, flowers, and herbs grew from her hair, and grass sprouted from her skin. Her eyes became small caves and springs; her mouth great rivers and caverns; and her nose the deep valleys and high mountains on land.

Aztec Religion

Religion was a very powerful force in the Aztec world, affecting everyone from the emperor right down to the most miserable slaves and prisoners. The Aztecs believed that the gods governed everything. It was pointless to go against their wishes, but it might sometimes be possible to influence them by making sacrifices and offerings.

Tlaloc

Tlaloc (left) was the Aztec god of rain and maize, the Aztecs' staple food. He was greatly feared because he was able to punish people by sending floods and droughts to destroy their crops. With his first wife, Xochiquetzal (sho-shee-KET-sal), Tlaloc ruled over Tlalocan (tla-low-CAN), the fourth Aztec heaven.

GODS AND GODDESSES

The Aztecs worshipped many different gods and goddesses. Some were ancient gods of nature who had been worshipped by the peoples of Mexico for thousands of years. Huitzilopochtli (weet-sill-oh-POSH-tlee), the Sun god and god of war, was also the Aztecs' tribal god. Without him, there would be no life on Earth.

Xipe Totec

Xipe Totec (shih-pay toh-tek), god of springtime, is shown here wearing the skin of a sacrificial victim. Priests would wear the skins of victims flayed alive in Xipe Totec's honor. This symbolized the spring plants which covered the Earth in a new "skin."

Quetzalcoatl

This turquoise mask shows Quetzalcoatl, the wind god who represented the forces of nature. Together with his brother, Tezcatlipoca, he was responsible for creating the world. He was also the inventor of books and the calendar, and the patron of priests.

OFFERINGS TO THE SUN GOD

To ensure that Huitzilopochtli rose each day in the sky, the Aztecs offered humans as sacrifices to him. These sacrifices took place in pyramid-shaped temples. They were presided over by priests and priestesses, their skin painted black to show their sacred role in society.

Mictlantecuhtli

Fearsome Mictlantecuhtli (Mick-tlahn-tay-COO-tlee) was the god of the dead and, in statues like this one, was shown as a skeleton. Those who died a natural death went to his kingdom of Mictlan, a cold and desperate underworld where he lived with his wife, Mictecacihuatl (mick-teckah-SEE-watl). He was associated with spiders, owls, and bats—the animals of the underworld.

THE RABBIT AND THE MOON

Following the creation of the new Earth and sky, the world remained in darkness, for the Fourth Sun had been destroyed in the flood. Many years passed in this way. Then, at last, the gods gathered at the ancient city of Teotihuacan (tay-oh-tee-WAH-kahn) to decide which of them would become the new Sun.

The great gods met in the gloom, their voices rising and falling in the darkness as they debated how to save the world. Which among them would carry the heavy burden of becoming the new Sun? Who would become the new Moon to provide light when the Sun did not?

After a long discussion, two of the gods stepped forward and volunteered to be sacrificed to become the Sun. One was Tecuciztecatl, who was rich, handsome, and horribly proud. The other was poor, ugly Nanahuatzin, his face disfigured by spots and sores. The two contenders could not have been more different, and the gods found it difficult to choose between them.

TRIALS OF THE GODS

Before the gods made their final decision, they set Tecuciztecatl and Nanahuatzin a series of tasks to prove their worth. Two great hills were built for them. Here, for four days and four nights, the two fasted and did penance while the gods prepared the huge sacrificial fire. These hills can still be seen at Teotihuacan today as the Pyramids of the Sun and the Moon.

During their fast, Tecuciztecatl and Nanahuatzin made offerings to the other gods. Even here, haughty Tecuciztecatl was determined to show off his wealth. He dressed in the finest robes imaginable, and his offerings were made from the finest materials. Instead of traditional fir branches, he offered costly quetzal feathers. Instead of grass balls, he offered gleaming gold spheres. And lastly, instead of cactus spines dipped in his own blood, he had exquisite slithers of jade, tipped with rich red coral. Even the

Above: The ruins of the Pyramid of the Moon at Teotihuacan in Mexico still stand today. According to Aztec legend, Teotihuacan was the place where the gods met to decide which of them would become the new Sun and Moon. Nanahuatzin became the Sun and Tecuciztecatl the Moon.

incense that he burned was of the rarest and highest quality. There was no way in which humble Nanahuatzin could match this extravagant display. Dressed in rags made from bark paper, all he had to offer were bundles of simple reeds in place of fir branches and grass balls. Jade and coral were far beyond his poor means so his cactus spines dripped with his own blood. For his incense, he picked scabs from the sores on his body. Tecuciztecatl laughed when he saw his rival's plight.

When the four days and nights were over, the gods led Tecuciztecatl and Nanahuatzin toward the blazing fire. Standing in a circle around the fire, they ordered Tecuciztecatl to jump into the burning flames.

"I shall obey," replied Tecuciztecatl, looking as if he did not have a care in the world.

He ran toward the fire but was driven back by the scorching heat. The next time he tried he was again not brave enough to take the last, long leap into the fire. Four times, Tecuciztecatl ran toward the fire, and four times he stopped and turned back. He was not as courageous as he thought.

Next the gods called Nanahuatzin and repeated their orders.

"I shall obey," Nanahuatzin replied.

He shut his eyes and took a deep breath to steady his nerves, then he ran fearlessly straight into the fire. The other gods watched in awe as his body crackled and sizzled in the flames. And so humble but courageous Nanahuatzin earned the right to become the new Sun. Tecuciztecatl, too, watched in amazement. He felt embarrassed and ashamed by his own cowardice, and he, too, rushed headlong into the flames and was burned.

An eagle and a jaguar followed the two gods into the ashes of the fire. And that is how the tips of the eagle's feathers came to be scorched black, and the jaguar's coat became smudged with black spots.

THE MOON AND THE SUN

After the fiery deaths of Tecuciztecatl and Nanahuatzin, the other gods waited anxiously for the first day of the new age to begin. Slowly but surely, the sky began to turn red all around. At last, dawn was breaking! The gods peered around and craned their necks to see where brave Nanahuatzin would appear. Then some of them pointed to the east and they watched in wonder as Nanahuatzin rose as the new Sun. No longer weak and sickly, he shone so brightly that the gods could not look at his face.

Not wishing to be outdone, Tecuciztecatl also rose into the sky, appearing as the new Moon. But he shone as brightly as the Sun, and the gods were worried that the Moon would outshine the Sun.

Immediately, one of the gods picked up a rabbit that was scampering by and threw it into the face of the Moon, thus dimming its light. And that is why the Moon shines less brightly than the Sun, and why to this day—if you look closely at the pattern of the craters and seas on its face—the Moon seems to bear markings in the shape of a rabbit.

HUMAN SACRIFICE

The Aztecs believed that, unless the gods were fed with human hearts and blood, they would die. If that happened, the Sun would no longer rise in the sky, the rain would no longer fall, and everything on Earth would die. Most sacrificial victims were prisoners of war, captured by the Aztecs in wars against neighboring states. These wars were known as Wars of Flowers and were fought solely to obtain captives to kill. Victims who were sacrificed were assured of a happy life after death. For four years, they were "companions of the Sun." They then returned to Earth in the form of butterflies or hummingbirds.

Below: These decorated stone and shell knives were found among the ruins of the Great Temple in Tenochtitlan. Knives such as these were used to kill victims of sacrifice.

THE PLUMED
SERPENT AND THE BONES

With the Sun at last restored in the sky, light returned to the world.
But there were still no human beings to live on the new Earth.
It was agreed that the Plumed Serpent, Quetzalcoatl, should brave
the trials of the underworld to bring back the materials needed to
make people. This was to prove a difficult and dangerous task,
as Mictlantecuhtli, the Lord of the Dead, did not take kindly
to intruders.

To make human beings, the gods needed the bones of the last people to have inhabited the Earth. These people had been turned into fish during the great flood that had ended the Fourth Sun. The trouble was that these precious bones were stored in Mictlan, the underworld, a realm of deadly darkness beneath the Earth. Here icy winds and dreadful demons waited to tear unfortunate visitors limb from limb. Worse still, to retrieve the bones meant facing Mictlantecuhtli, the terrifying Lord of the Dead. Even a glimpse of Mictlantecuhtli was enough to scare a person to death. Dressed in clothes made from strips of bark paper, Mictlantecuhtli looked like a skeleton with black, curly hair that sparkled with stars. Very few survived being caught in Mictlantecuhtli's huge, clawlike hands.

THE SEARCH FOR THE BONES

Only one god was considered brave enough to face Mictlantecuhtli in his own kingdom, and that was Quetzalcoatl, god of the wind. Quetzalcoatl was happy to oblige, and so he descended into the gloom of the underworld, accompanied by his faithful dog, Xolotl (SHO-lotl), god of monsters. Even entering Mictlan was fraught with danger, and Quetzalcoatl had to undergo a series of terrible ordeals. First, he was almost burned to death and only managed to escape by transforming himself into a bird. Then, he faced the threat of beheading but saved himself by turning into a star.

Finally, in the darkest, most dreadful part of Mictlan, Quetzalcoatl came face to face with Mictlantecuhtli himself. He asked him for the bones of the fish-people.

"But what will you do with them, Quetzalcoatl?" cackled Mictlantecuhtli, cracking his bony knuckles. "Why should I give the bones to you? Tell me that, if you dare."

"We, the gods, have made a new world," Quetzalcoatl replied. "And we are anxious to fill it with people again. I will make people from the bones you give me. You must hand them over to me—it is your destiny."

But the devious Lord of Death did not intend to part with the bones so easily. Using all of his cunning, he set Quetzalcoatl what he considered to be an impossible task.

Right: A drawing of the god Quetzalcoatl from the Codex Borbonicus. In Aztec mythology, Quetzalcoatl had to brave many terrible trials in the underworld and outwit Mictlantecuhtli, god of death, to make the creation of human beings possible.

"You must travel four times around the underworld," Mictlantecuhtli told Quetzalcoatl, "while blowing a conch shell trumpet."

It sounded like a simple thing to do—but the conch shell Mictlantecuhtli gave to Quetzalcoatl did not have any holes in it. It could not make a sound, no matter how hard Quetzalcoatl blew. Not to be outwitted, Quetzalcoatl called on some underworld worms to drill holes in the conch shell, and a swarm of bees to fly inside. Now, when he blew on the shell, it made a loud and distinctive buzzing sound.

Hearing the blasts from the conch shell, Mictlantecuhtli knew that the time had come to hand over the bones. He could not delay any longer. But he bitterly resented parting with them and, as soon as he had given the bones to Quetzalcoatl, he set about trying to trick him into giving them up again.

As Quetzalcoatl made his way out of the underworld, Mictlantecuhtli ordered his demons to dig a deep pit right across his path. When Quetzalcoatl drew near, a flock of quails flew right in front of his face. Startled, Quetzalcoatl stumbled into the pit, dropping the bag of bones. When the god pulled himself out of the hole and picked up the scattered bones, he found that many of them were broken into pieces, some large and some small. Those bones that were not already shattered were being picked at by

Left: With her frightening appearance and terrible teeth, Mictecacihuatl, the wife of Mictlantecuhtli, kept watch over the bones of the dead, and presided over the festivals of the dead in the underworld.

LIFE AFTER DEATH

The Aztecs believed in a heaven and an underworld. There were thirteen levels of heaven and nine of the underworld. Where your soul went after death depended on how you had died, rather than on the manner in which you had lived. Warriors who died in battle and victims of sacrifice went to Tonatiuh (ton-a-TEE-oo), the heaven of the Sun. But most people went to Mictlan, the underworld. The journey through the nine levels to Mictlan was difficult and took four years to complete. It involved nine trials for the soul to undergo, including crossing a deep river, being blown by an icy wind, being pierced by arrows, and battling with wild beasts. To make the trip, people were buried in a squatting position with items to help them on their way. These included water, and offerings for Mictlantecuhtli. A dog was also needed to guide the soul through the underworld, so a dog was sacrificed as part of funeral rites.

the quails. And that is why the people Quetzalcoatl later made came in a variety of different shapes and sizes.

A NEW PEOPLE

Having escaped from the underworld, brave Quetzalcoatl carried the bag of bones to the gods. They had gathered in the heaven of Tamoanchan (tam-oh-AN-chan) to wait for him to return.

Quetzalcoatl gave the bones to the old mother goddess, Cihuacoatl (see-wah-COH-atl), who ground them into a fine powder which she put in a special pot. Then she asked the gods for some of their blood.

The gods gathered around the pot, and pricked their tongues and earlobes with thorns so that their blood dripped onto the powder. Then Cihuacoatl mixed the powder and the blood together to make a thick paste.

The gods watched and waited to see what would happen. They had to be patient. Then, finally, after four days, a little boy appeared out of the paste. After four more days, a little girl appeared. And so human beings were made from the bones of the fish-people and the blood of the gods.

THE RED
ANT AND THE MAIZE

Although people had now returned to the Earth, there was nothing for them to eat. All of the gods went off in search of food to keep people alive and to give them strength. Once again, though, it was the god of wind, Quetzalcoatl, who saved the day. He managed to find the source of maize, which became the Aztecs' staple food, and of pulque (POOL-kay), their favorite drink.

The gods set off in all four directions from the heaven of Tamoanchan to find food. They traveled across the Earth for days, searching high and low, but they could not find anything suitable. Then one day, the god Quetzalcoatl spotted a red ant carrying a kernel of maize.

"Where did this food come from?" he asked the ant.

The ant refused to tell him and scurried quickly away. Curious, Quetzalcoatl followed the ant until it reached mighty Mount Tonacatepetl (ton-a-KAT-eh-petal), the mythical Mountain of Sustenance. Then he watched as the red ant disappeared through a minute crack in the rock. What was hidden inside the mountain? And why was it so precious that it was kept a secret? Quetzalcoatl was determined to find out. Quick as a flash, he transformed himself into a tiny black ant, and followed the red ant deep inside the mountain. To Quetzalcoatl's astonishment, the ant led him to a chamber filled to the roof with piles of seeds and grain.

Quetzalcoatl picked up some of the kernels of maize and carried them back to Tamoanchan, where the gods were waiting.

"What have you brought us, Quetzalcoatl?" they asked. "It had better taste good, whatever it is. People are getting hungry."

When the gods tasted some of the kernels of maize, they found that it tasted very good indeed. They ground some maize up to make a mash and gave it to the human

FARMING AND FOOD

Aztec farmers worked hard to raise crops for food and tribute. In different parts of the empire, farmers cultivated their land in different ways. In the south, they cleared small fields in the dense rain forest. Here, they grew cacao beans (for making drinking chocolate), papayas, and pineapples. In the dry, dusty highlands, they cut terraces into the hillsides to increase the available farmland. Here, they grew maize, the Aztecs' staple food, beans, and squashes. Farmers also created "gardens" called *chinampas* in and around swampy lakes. The gardens were made from rich, dark mud dredged from the lake floor. This mud was extremely fertile and produced huge crops.

Left: This illustration shows Aztecs building a *chinampa*. First, a narrow strip was staked out in the lake. Then the chinampa was built up with thick mats of lake vegetation and mud. Willow trees were planted around the edge of the chinampa to hold it together.

babies to eat. And the babies grew healthy and strong, much to the gods' delight. They decreed that everyone should have some of this nourishing new food. But how were they going to get the maize out of its mountainous hiding place?

SPLITTING THE MOUNTAIN

For several days, the gods debated what they should do. Then Quetzalcoatl had an idea. He tied a great rope around the mountain and attempted to drag it off. But even mighty Quetzalcoatl was not strong enough to make the mountain move.

The gods turned to an old man and woman called Oxomoco (oh-shoh-MOH-coh) and Cipactonal (see-pack-TOH-nal) for advice. Oxomoco and Cipactonal had the power to see into the future. The gods asked them how they could get to the food hidden inside

Above and left: The Aztecs worshipped a number of maize deities, linked to different stages of the plant's growth. Xilonen (shi-LOW-nen; above), "Young Ear of Maize," was goddess of the first, tender shoots of corn. Chicomecoatl (chee-koh-may-KOH-atl; left), "Seven Snake," was linked to the maize harvest. At Chicomecoatl's festival in April or May, the Aztecs decorated their homes with ears of corn and the priests blessed the stores of maize in the temples.

Mount Tonacatepetl. Oxomoco and Cipactonal thought long and hard, before declaring that the gods should call on Nanahuatzin, the god who had become the Fifth Sun. He would be able to help them.

So the gods summoned Nanahuatzin. And, as Oxomoco and Cipactonal had prophesied, he helped them to get the food out. Assisted by the four gods of rain and lightning   the blue, red, white, and yellow Tlalocs—Nanahuatzin split Mount Tonacatepetl wide open, scattering the maize kernels and other seeds all around. Quickly, the Tlalocs snatched up some maize seeds, as well as the seeds of beans and other plants. After retrieving these seeds at Tonacatepetl, the Tlalocs became the gods of the crops that people grew in their fields, as well as of the rain that nourishes them.

THE SACRED DRINK

Although people now had plenty of food, there was little in their lives that made them happy. As Quetzalcoatl watched them going about their daily tasks, he noticed that they never danced or sang. They needed something to raise their spirits, and Quetzalcoatl thought that he had the very thing—a delicious drink that they could all enjoy. At once, he set off through the thirteen heavens until he met Mayahuel (my-AH-well), the bewitchingly beautiful goddess of the maguey cactus plant. Quetzalcoatl and Mayahuel fell madly in love, and Quetzalcoatl led her with him back down to Earth. There, as a sign of their devotion, they turned themselves into a great two-forked tree with Quetzalcoatl as one branch and Mayahuel as the other.

Unfortunately, Mayahuel was also the granddaughter of one of the wicked night demons who constantly threatened to destroy the world. When her grandmother discovered that Mayahuel was missing, she was furious. She followed the couple to Earth with an army of terrible demons, bringers of misery and woe.

The demons swept across the sky like a storm, along ancient paths of darkness, until they spied the great tree. As they swooped down, the tree split in half and the two branches crashed to the ground. The demons poured down to take their revenge. Shrieking hideously, they tore the body of Mayahuel apart and gobbled the pieces up. Then they were gone, as quickly as they came.

Heartbroken, Quetzalcoatl gathered up Mayahuel's bones and buried them in the ground. As he dug her grave, he wept tears of grief which watered the Earth. And in time, the first maguey cactus plant sprouted up from Mayahuel's grave. From the sap of the maguey, people learned to make a drink, called pulque, which quickly became their favorite.

Snow-capped Popocatepetl (pop-oh-KAT-eh-petal) stands about 40 miles (70 km) to the southeast of present-day Mexico City. According to Aztec legend, Popocatepetl was a warrior who fell in love with a beautiful princess. After her death, the warrior was so grief-stricken that he killed himself and the gods turned him into a mountain.

Tales of the Aztec Gods

A good harvest, victory in war, health and prosperity, and even the rising of the Sun itself, depended, the Aztecs believed, on the will of the gods. The Aztecs worshipped a bewildering number of gods and goddesses. Some were ancient deities; others were adopted from civilizations that the Aztecs conquered. They believed that the gods and goddesses were created by the god Ometeotl, who took the forms of the female Omecihuatl (oh-mey-SEE-watl) and the male Ometecuhtli (oh-meh-tay-COO-tlee), the mother and father deities. Legend says that Omecihuatl gave birth to 1,600 gods and goddesses. This number was not meant to be an exact calculation but to suggest a number so huge that it was "beyond counting." Each of the Aztec deities could take many different guises. The god Quetzalcoatl, for example, could be the Plumed Serpent and the wind god Ehecatl, among many other forms.

In their everyday lives, the Aztecs consulted the gods in all they did and performed numerous rituals and ceremonies to try to win the gods' favor. They also told many stories of the trials, tribulations, and adventures of the gods.

THE PLACE OF THE CACTUS

The Aztecs had not always lived in the Valley of Mexico. Their ancestors emerged, long ago, from one of the sacred seven caves of Chicomoztoc (chee-koh-MOZ-tok) in the region of Aztlan ("Land of the Cranes"), a dry, barren place somewhere in the far north. From this place, they set out on a long, wandering journey into the Valley of Mexico in search of a land they could make their home. But they were not alone in their trek. At every step, they were guided by Huitzilopochtli, the great god of war.

From the first moment of his life, the god of war, Huitzilopochtli, was destined to be a great warrior. It is said that he was born fully armed. His mother was the earth goddess, Coatlicue (koh-ah-TLEEK-way), who was known by her skirt of serpents, and was priestess of a shrine high up on the mountainside at Coatepec (koh-ah-THE-pek), near the ancient city of Tollan. One day, as Coatlicue was sweeping the shrine, she spotted a ball of brightly colored hummingbird feathers. Rather than throwing the feathers away, she tucked them into her belt. While she worked, she forgot all about the feathers. But when she looked for them later, they had disappeared. Soon afterward, Coatlicue discovered that the ball of feathers had miraculously made her pregnant.

THE BIRTH OF HUITZILOPOCHTLI

Coatlicue already had one daughter, the Moon goddess Coyolxauhqui (koy-yoll-SHAU-kee), and 400 warlike sons, called the Centzonhuitznahuac (sent-son-weets-NAH-wak). When Coatlicue's daughter and sons found out that she was pregnant, they were so angry that they decided to kill her. High up in her mountain shrine, a terrified Coatlicue heard their voices rising and falling as they plotted her death. Then she heard another voice, coming from deep inside her.

"Do not be afraid," the voice said. "The child that is about to be born will protect you from harm."

Dressed for battle, the Centzonhuitznahuac followed their sister to Coatepec. Knives ready, they climbed up the mountainside to their mother's shrine. But, just as they were about to attack her, Huitzilopochtli was born, already dressed in his warrior's garb. His face, arms, and legs were painted bright blue, and he wore plumes of hummingbird feathers on his head and left leg. In one hand, he carried a shield decorated with eagle's feathers; in the other, he held the flaming fire-serpent which guided the Sun across the sky. Wielding this mighty weapon, he killed Coyolxauhqui and cut her body into pieces that tumbled down the mountainside. Next, he killed many of his brothers, allowing a few shell-shocked survivors to escape to the south.

Huitzilopochtli became the great god of the Aztecs, and their guide and protector. On his orders, the Aztecs left their humble origins in Aztlan and began the long journey to the Valley of Mexico in search of a place to live.

WAR AND WARRIORS

The Aztecs' power was based on warfare, and war was a normal part of Aztec life. The Aztecs went to war to enlarge their empire and to capture prisoners to sacrifice to the gods. The highest aim of an Aztec man was to be a successful warrior and he was expected to be brave, noble, and respectful of the gods. Warriors who showed particular courage in battle were rewarded with high social rank and land. The Aztec emperor, priests, and nobles were the chief war leaders. The bravest nobles were allowed to join one of two prestigious military orders—the Eagle Knights and the Jaguar Knights—which combined fighting skills with religious vows. Dressed in eagle or jaguar costumes, they were the most highly regarded soldiers in the Aztec army and led the army into war.

Right: This life-sized clay sculpture shows an Aztec eagle warrior, dressed in an eagle helmet and armor. It was found guarding a doorway to a chamber next to the Great Temple in Tenochtitlan, where the Eagle Knights met. In Aztec culture, the eagle was the symbol of the Sun, and the Eagle Knights were the Soldiers of the Sun.

THE GREAT JOURNEY

As Huitzilopochtli had foretold, seven peoples emerged from the seven caves at Chicomoztoc and left the region of Aztlan, one by one. But the Aztecs were not allowed to leave immediately. As the first six peoples were leaving, Huitzilopochtli ordered the Aztecs to stay behind and light a ceremonial fire—a sign that great things were about to happen. It was not until many years later that the Aztecs set out on their great journey.

Leading the trek were four god-bearers, known for their devotion. They carried a glittering gold statue of Huitzilopochtli and interpreted the pronouncements he made. Every day, the god spoke to the Aztecs to tell them which route to take. When Huitzilopochtli told them to move on or to stop, they obeyed him.

The Aztecs traveled southward across the dry, cactus lands. Not far into their journey, they came to a beautiful garden, filled with exquisitely perfumed flowers and shaded by an enormous tree. It looked like the perfect place for the Aztecs to settle down. In high spirits, they built a shrine to Huitzilopochtli and celebrated the end of their journey with a sumptuous feast. Then disaster struck. As they sat eating, the great tree split in two with a deafening crack. This was an omen of the worst possible kind.

Left: An illustration from a sixteenth-century Aztec codex shows part of the Aztecs' long journey to Lake Texcoco. It was drawn on fig bark paper.

The Aztecs were horrified. Trembling with fear, they gathered in a circle to hear what Huitzilopochtli would say.

"You must leave this place at once," he told them, in his twittering, birdlike voice. "Continue on your journey. It is no longer safe for you to stay here."

The Aztecs wept at the thought of leaving this paradise behind. With heavy hearts, they set out again on their wanderings, following the god-bearers. They stopped many times on the way. In some places, they stayed for twenty years or more, building temples and even ball courts. In other places, they laid out fields and grew maize, chilis, beans, and other crops. They hunted for animals in the forests, and captured human victims to sacrifice to the gods. But eventually, they always moved on, as Huitzilopochtli ordered them to. And if old and sick people could not keep up, they were left behind.

Finally, after 100 long years of traveling, Huitzilopochtli led the Aztecs to the shores of Lake Texcoco. They settled on a hill called Chapultepec (chah-PULL-the-pek), where a spring of fresh water gushed up from the rocks. In their new home, they came under the rule of the king of Culhuacan (kull-wah-KAHN) and served him for a while as soldiers. But they were not welcome in his kingdom for long. One day, on Huitzilopochtli's orders, the Aztecs kidnapped the king's daughter and sacrificed her to the gods. When he found out what they had done, the king was beside himself with grief, and the Aztecs were forced to flee for their lives. Under cover of night, they went into hiding among the reed beds and swampy marshes that fringed the lake.

THE EAGLE AND THE CACTUS

Next morning, before the Sun rose, the Aztecs loaded up their canoes and paddled off to a group of islands in the middle of the lake. As they reached the shore, one of the god-bearers was almost blinded by a dazzling vision of Huitzilopochtli.

"Look for a place where an eagle is perched on a cactus," the god told him. "The eagle will be holding a snake in its talons. This is where you must build your city, and where you will find wealth and glory."

So overcome was the god-bearer by what he had seen and heard that he shook uncontrollably and collapsed on the ground. The other god-bearers pulled him to his feet and asked him what the matter was, for they had not seen Huitzilopochtli themselves. But the god-bearer could only mutter:

"Look for a cactus and an eagle! This is the place! This is the place!" Astonished, the Aztecs gazed around at their damp and misty surroundings. Could this inhospitable place really be the spot promised to them by Huitzilopochtli? Then suddenly, a great shout

Right: This illustration is found at the front of the famous Codex Mendoza, which was created in 1541–1542, two decades after the Spanish conquest of Mexico. It shows the Aztecs paying homage to the eagle and cactus which became the emblem of their new city of Tenochtitlan. The crossed blue bands represent the canals that divided the city into four quarters.

went up. There, perched on a prickly pear cactus, was an enormous eagle holding a snake—the sign they had been waiting for. At that moment, the Aztecs saw the Sun rise in the sky and watched its light fall on the spot, a sign of blessing from their great god and leader. They threw themselves to the ground, praising and thanking Huitzilopochtli. Around the cactus, they built a temple in which they placed the statue they had carried with them throughout their long wanderings. As they built, they found springs of red and blue water, which were a sign that the place was blessed.

And so the Aztecs built a great city on the site chosen by Huitzilopochtli. They called their city Tenochtitlan ("Place of the Prickly Pear") and it was the site of the present-day Mexico City.

Tenochtitlan

Guided by Huitzilopochtli, the Aztecs built the great city of Tenochtitlan on an island in Lake Texcoco. At first, Tenochtitlan was simply a huddle of huts made from woven reeds. But from its humble beginnings, the city grew to a great size. By the time the Spanish arrived in 1519, it was home to almost 200,000 people and the capital of a mighty empire that stretched from the east coast of Mexico to the west.

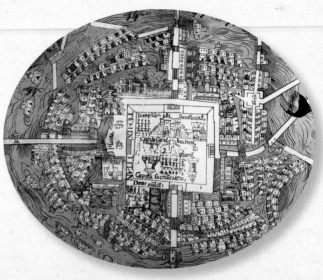

Above: This sixteenth-century map of Tenochtitlan was drawn for the Spanish leader, Hernando Cortés, to illustrate a letter to the Holy Roman Emperor, Charles V (1500–1558). It clearly shows the causeways linking the city to the mainland.

CANALS AND CAUSEWAYS

Tenochtitlan was situated on the western side of Lake Texcoco, and covered some 7 square miles (18 sq km). It was connected to the mainland by three gigantic causeways, and crisscrossed with a network of canals for transport by canoe. Laid out on a grid pattern, the city was divided into four zones, each divided further into twenty districts, called *calpullis*. Each *calpulli* had its own marketplace where the Aztecs could buy everything from precious stones and jaguar skins to firewood and salt.

Above: This panel of stone skulls was found at the site of the Great Temple in Tenochtitlan. Real skulls were placed on a skull rack outside Aztec temples. They were usually the skulls of victims who had been sacrificed to the gods.

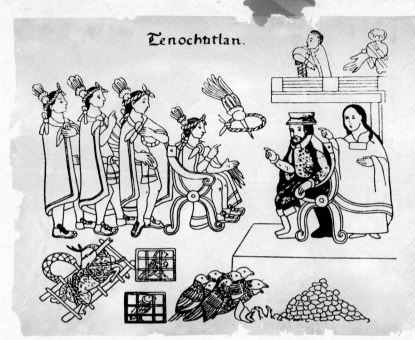

Tenochtitlan.

Left: A sixteenth-century illustration records the meeting between the Aztec emperor, Moctezuma II (c. 1466–1520), and Hernando Cortés in Tenochtitlan in 1519. When they first met, Moctezuma sent Cortés gifts, thinking that he was the god Quetzalcoatl returning from exile. He quickly realized how wrong he had been.

SACRED PRECINCT

In the center of the city stood the sacred precinct. Surrounded by a stone wall some 1,300 feet (400 m) high, entry was limited to nobles and foreign dignitaries. Inside stood the magnificent Great Temple, dedicated to the gods Huitzilopochtli and Tlaloc. Around this were several other temples, a ball court, a skull rack, and a large, circular stone where poorly armed prisoners of war fought to the death against the mighty Aztec warriors.

Right: The final battle between Cortés and the new Aztec emperor, Cuauhtemoc (kwow-TAY-mok; c. 1502–1525), took place in Tenochtitlan in August 1521. Tenochtitlan was destroyed and Cuauhtemoc was caught trying to escape. Mexico City was later built on the site.

copolco
Zoimicca y
capitan.

TEZCATLIPOCA AND THE
KING of TOLLAN

From the beginning of the first creation, the god Tezcatlipoca had been a bringer of evil and discord in the world. As god of the night, Tezcatlipoca was believed to roam the Earth in the dark, looking for victims to capture for sacrifice. He was never to be trusted and often misused his great powers to spread conflict and mayhem. The Toltec people of Tollan had particular cause to be afraid of his tricky and dangerous nature.

Tezcatlipoca was also known as the Lord of the Smoking Mirror. Long ago, according to legend, a mirror was made from smoke-colored glass, and this mirror could predict when there would be famine. A time came when the crops failed and people were starving. Wicked Tezcatlipoca stole the glass mirror and hid it so that people would continue to suffer long after they needed to. After that, he used the mirror to take the place of the foot he had lost when the gods threw him out of the thirteenth heaven. Using his smoking mirror, which reflected the night even when it was daytime, Tezcatlipoca could see into the future and into the most hidden places of people's hearts. Worst of all, the mirror gave Tezcatlipoca control over the forces of destruction.

THE CHILI SELLER

On one occasion, Tezcatlipoca traveled to the city of Tollan, intent on causing trouble. Dressed in rags and with his body painted bright green, he made his way to the marketplace, where he pretended to be a poor seller of chilis.

Cunning Tezcatlipoca knew that the King of Tollan had a daughter whose beauty was famous far and wide. Every day, offers of marriage arrived but the king would not allow the princess to accept any of these suitors. One day, the princess went to

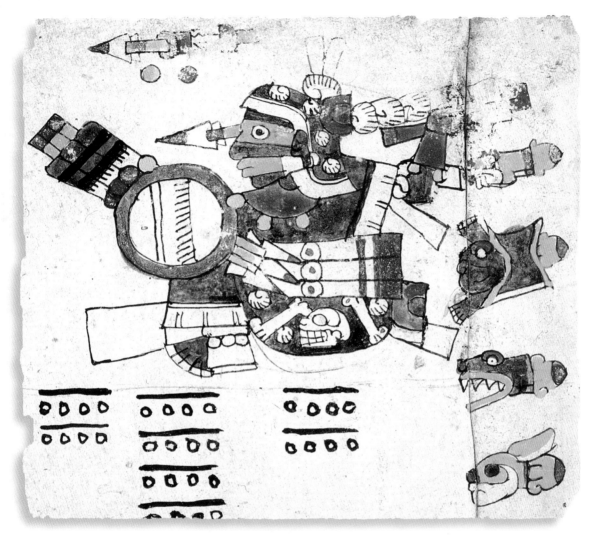

Above: A page from the Codex Cospi shows the god Tezcatlipoca in his guise as the bringer of war. He is armed and dressed as a warrior, with his robes decorated with a skull and bones. On the battlefield, he decided which warriors should succeed and which fall.

market, where she caught sight of the chili seller. Without saying a word, Tezcatlipoca was able to work his magic on her and she immediately fell madly in love with him, as he knew she would. Day after day, she longed for another glimpse of the chili seller, and pined so much that she became ill. Anxious for his daughter, the king asked her maidservants what was wrong. They told him about the princess's love for the stranger who had stolen her heart.

THE TOLTECS

Toltec civilization flourished from c. 900 to 1200 C.E. Toltec society was led by priest-kings, associated with the god Quetzalcoatl. The Toltecs were master builders and artists, and also great warriors. Their magnificent capital city was Tollan, which lay about 50 miles (80 km) to the north of Tenochtitlan and was much admired by the Aztecs.

Tollan had splendid palaces, vast squares, and towering temples. Its main temple was famous far and wide for its walls covered in sheets of gold, seashells, and precious stones. Equally famous was the House of Feathers, whose rooms were decorated with the feathers of rare birds. Around 1200 C.E., the Toltecs were defeated by the Chichimec people and Tollan was destroyed. However, much information about the Toltecs was preserved in Aztec poems, which were passed down the generations orally, then written down after the Spanish conquest.

Left: These magnificent stone figures of Toltec warriors helped to support the main temple at Tollan. Firebirds, symbols of the Toltec ruling classes, were carved on their chests. The Toltecs were great warriors, as shown by the many warrior statues that have survived.

The king sent out his soldiers to search for the chili seller. They found him, dirty and wild-looking, in the marketplace and led him back to the palace. It was exactly as Tezcatlipoca had planned. As soon as the princess set eyes on the beloved ragged stranger, she was completely cured of her illness. The king, however, was horrified when he saw the chili seller. This was not the sort of husband he had imagined for his daughter. But he was so relieved to see her well again that he gave his blessing for the two of them to get married.

Not everyone in Tollan was pleased to hear of the marriage. "Has the king gone mad," the people of the city wondered, "to let the princess marry this crazy-looking man?"

Furious about being laughed at, the king began to plot a means of getting rid of his new son-in-law. He launched a war against Tollan's enemies and sent the chili seller to fight alongside his men.

On the king's orders, the soldiers sent the chili seller right into the middle of the battlefield, where the fighting was at its fiercest. They hoped that he would be killed, but their plan backfired. To their astonishment, the chili seller fought very bravely and won the admiration of the whole army.

DANCE OF DEATH

News of the chili seller's courage reached Tollan and, on his return to the city, he was greeted as a hero. Crowds lined the streets to cheer him home, as he proudly paraded in the quetzal feather headdress of a great warrior, with his beautiful wife on his arm. Even the king was forced to admit that he was glad to have the chili seller as his son-in-law.

But the unsuspecting people of Tollan could have no idea what Tezcatlipoca had planned for them. To celebrate his homecoming, he invited them all to a fabulous feast in the public square. Everyone crowded in enthusiastically. Then Tezcatlipoca began to sing, and made the people dance along to the music. The faster Tezcatlipoca sang, the faster the people danced.

Faster and faster he sang until people were dancing so quickly that they began to feel dizzy and weak. And still Tezcatlipoca would not stop. He sang faster and faster until they could no longer stay on their feet. Helplessly, they plummeted into a crack in the ground that the god had caused to open up.

Over and over they tumbled until all of the people had fallen down dead and the city of Tollan was destroyed.

The Aztec World

Above: A portrait of Moctezuma II, who was elected emperor in 1502. He was the ruler of the Aztec Empire at the time of the Spanish conquest. Moctezuma allowed the Spanish to enter Tenochtitlan in 1519, and was held hostage by Hernando Cortés. He was killed in 1520 by a rock thrown either by his own people or by the Spanish.

In less than 200 years, the Aztecs were transformed from a humble nomadic people to supreme rulers of the Valley of Mexico. From their capital, Tenochtitlan, the Aztecs conquered many neighboring towns and cities, which paid them tribute. At its greatest extent, the Aztec empire stretched from the Pacific to the Atlantic coasts.

THE EMPEROR AND THE GOVERNMENT

The most important person in Aztec society was the emperor, known as the Huei Tlatoani (way tlah-toh-AAH-nee), which means "Great Speaker." He was elected by a council of priests, nobles, and generals. The Tlatoani lived in a sumptuous palace in the heart of Tenochtitlan, surrounded by officials, servants, and wives. He was head of the government and leader of the army. After his election, he had to prove his worth as leader by taking an army into battle.

A second great official, known as "Snake Woman," acted as the Tlatoani's deputy. Despite the title, the post was always held by a man. He ran the day-to-day affairs of the government.

Right: A codex drawing shows the ceremonial costumes worn by Aztec knights and nobles as they led the army into war. The Aztecs fought many wars with their neighbors to ensure new territories for their expanding empire and a steady supply of tribute and captives for sacrificing to the gods.

AZTEC SOCIETY

Aztec society was divided into different classes, or ranks. At the top were the emperor and his immediate family. Beneath the emperor were the nobles. These included government officials, and rulers of cities that paid tribute to the emperor. Many nobles rose to their privileged positions by being priests. Below the nobles came the commoners, the majority of the population who mostly made their living by farming. Below them was a class of laborers who could be hired for work. At the bottom were the slaves, many of whom were criminals or had been captured in war. Only the emperor and nobles could wear fine cloth, precious feathers, and gold ornaments. Ordinary people had to wear clothes made from the rough fibers of the maguey cactus plant.

Left: In an Aztec family, the father worked to support the family while the mother looked after the household and cared for the children. This scene from the Codex Mendoza shows an Aztec mother teaching her children to make tortillas.

THE FALL OF THE
FLOWER GODDESS

The goddesses of the Earth provided the Aztecs with crops for food, and materials for building and making clothes—all the necessities of life. One of these Earth goddesses was the beautiful Xochiquetzal (sho-shee-KET-sal), the flower goddess. Her gift to the people of the world was the sweet-smelling flowers that grew by the wayside. Every eight years, a great feast was held in her honor at which people dressed up in animal and flower masks.

Xochiquetzal, whose name meant "Precious Flower Feather," ruled Tamoanchan, the thirteenth level of heaven. She had been created by the gods Tezcatlipoca and Quetzalcoatl at the beginning of the world. Dressed in a headdress of shimmering quetzal feathers, she held a flower and a butterfly in her hands. In her gorgeous paradise, high above the Earth, it was summer all year round. Birds sang and flowers bloomed. In the center of the heaven grew a massive tree whose branches were heavy with blossoms and fruit. It was in heavenly Tamoanchan that the gods created the first people from the bones they rescued from the underworld. And it was here that Xochiquetzal lived with her followers, who flitted around in the form of brightly colored birds and butterflies.

Xochiquetzal was the first wife of Tlaloc, the great god of rain, and they lived very happily. Only once had their happiness been threatened. The wicked god of the night, Tezcatlipoca, had become infatuated with Xochiquetzal's beauty and charm. He tried to win her over with his magic tricks and good looks, but to his fury, she only had eyes for her husband. So jealous Tezcatlipoca took drastic action. He kidnapped Xochiquetzal and carried her off to the dark depths of the underworld. Luckily, she managed to escape when he was not looking and made her way back to Tamoanchan.

TREE OF TEMPTATION

Surrounded by her loyal handmaidens, Xochiquetzal spent her days laughing and singing. As goddess of weaving, she made cloth in many wonderful colors and patterns, while jugglers, acrobats, and dancers kept her entertained. Xochiquetzal lived an enchanted life, or so it seemed. One day, however, disaster struck in paradise.

The flowers and fruits that grew on the great tree in the middle of Tamoanchan were the most beautiful that had ever been seen. The flowers were sweet-smelling, and the round, red fruits looked ripe and delicious to eat. Birds were allowed to build their nests on the great tree's branches, and squirrels and other animals scampered up and down its trunk. But the supreme god, Ometeotl, gave the gods and goddesses of Tamoanchan a solemn order. None of them was permitted to pick the flowers or taste the fruit of the tree, and that included Xochitquetzal. Even though she was ruler of Tamoanchan, she still had to obey the great Ometeotl's orders.

Right: This fifteenth-century seated stone figure of the flower goddess, Xochiquetzal, shows her wearing a headdress decorated with blooms.

Left: Goldsmiths enjoyed a high status in Aztec society. They made intricate objects, such as this beautiful figure of an Aztec bird god, using the "lost wax" method. Molten gold was poured into a beeswax mold covered in clay. As the gold poured in, the wax melted and trickled out.

The trouble was that Xochiquetzal was entranced by the tree. Every day, she sat underneath its spreading branches and enjoyed its soothing shade. And every day, she would study its flowers and fruit, longing to pick them. One day, she could bear the temptation no longer. Even though she knew it was not allowed, she picked some of the flowers to make a garland for her hair, and plucked some ripe, red fruits to eat.

ARTS AND CRAFTS

As well as being goddess of flowers, Xochiquetzal was also the goddess of artists and craftworkers, such as weavers, silversmiths, and painters. In Aztec society, professional craftworkers were divided into groups, called guilds. The most respected were the feather-workers who used feathers from tropical birds, such as quetzals, to make exquisite cloaks and headdresses for high-ranking nobles and warriors. Goldsmiths were also highly valued for their beautiful gold jewelry and figurines. Although thousands of these objects were made, very few have survived. In their greed for gold, the Spanish melted many of these works of arts down and used the gold to make coins.

Xochiquetzal hoped that no one would notice what she had done. After all, there were hundreds of flowers and fruits on the tree's branches. Surely the few that she had taken would not be missed?

But Xochiquetzal had disobeyed Ometeotl, and Ometeotl saw everything. As Xochiquetzal sat underneath it, the great tree began to shudder and shake. Then, with a terrible creaking sound, it split and splintered into pieces. A horrified Xochiquetzal saw that there was blood oozing from the places on the tree where she had picked the fruit and flowers.

BANISHED FROM HEAVEN

Looking on, the great Ometeotl was greatly disturbed. He loved Xochiquetzal for her beauty and charm, but he also knew that she had to be punished for disobeying his orders.

With a heavy heart, Ometeotl summoned Xochiquetzal to his presence and informed her of her fate. It was worse than anything she could possibly have imagined. Ometeotl banished the foolish Xochiquetzal from her home in heaven and sent her down to live among the mountains and plains on Earth, where she spent the rest of her life.

And every time she passed a beautiful flower, her eyes spilled over with tears at the thought of all the wonderful things she had lost.

Surrounded by tropical rain forest, the mysterious
Temple of the Inscriptions stands among the
ruins of the Maya city of Palenque in Mexico.
Its nine levels symbolized the nine levels of
the Maya underworld.

Maya Creation Myths

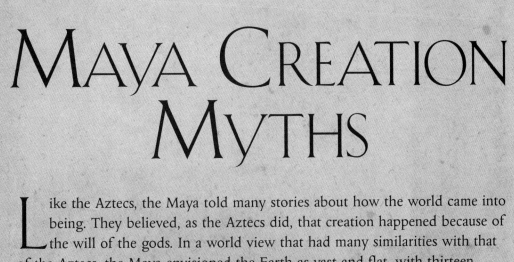

Like the Aztecs, the Maya told many stories about how the world came into being. They believed, as the Aztecs did, that creation happened because of the will of the gods. In a world view that had many similarities with that of the Aztecs, the Maya envisioned the Earth as vast and flat, with thirteen levels of heaven above and nine layers of underworld beneath. At each of the four corners of the Earth grew a tree that held up the sky. In some versions of the myths, giants took the place of the trees. In the center of the Earth stood a greater tree, which joined heaven, the Earth, and the underworld.

The following series of creation myths tells the story of how the gods formed the Earth and the animals, how they then created people at their third attempt, and how, finally, they created the Sun and the Moon.

THE CONVERSATION
OF THE GODS

Before time began, there only existed a great, still expanse of sea and sky. There were no animals, plants, or people. There were no rocks, plains, or forests. There was nothing that could make a noise, and nothing that could move. There was only the great sea god, Gucumatz (goo-koo-mahts), and the great sky god, Huracan (hoo-rah-kan). In the silence, an extraordinary conversation started up between the two of them, and from their conversation the Earth and everything on it was created.

In the sea, the god Gucumatz, the Plumed Serpent, shimmered and glittered in the water. He lay coiled beneath the waves, surrounded by glimmering blue and green quetzal feathers. At the same time, in the sky above, the god Huracan, known as the Heart of Heaven, appeared as a shining streak of lightning. In the darkness and stillness, the two gods began to talk to each other, debating and deliberating long into the night.

CREATING THE EARTH

During their conversation, Gucumatz and Huracan planned the creation of the Earth, the dawning of the first day, and the making of people and their food. They created a vision of what the Earth should look like, how plants and trees should grow in the soil, how the Sun and Moon should move in the sky, and how animals and people should live.

"Let it be done!" they said. "Let the emptiness be filled! Let the waters of the sea be pushed back to make space for the Earth to appear. Let there be light, let there be a dawn in the sky and on Earth. Then let human beings be formed!"

As the gods spoke, their words had a magical and immediate effect. The waters of the sea were pushed back, and the Earth rose up. Steep-sided mountains appeared from the water and grew instantly. Forests covered the landscape, and plants sprouted in the fields. Water collected in hollows to make the great lakes, and flowed down the sides of the mountains in raging rivers and babbling streams.

Gucumatz and Huracan looked at their work and were overjoyed. But there was still one part of creation missing. The gods needed creatures who would thank and praise them for all their great work. So they decided to create the birds and animals of the land, hoping that they would honor the gods.

Right: A stone head of the Plumed Serpent, Gucumatz, stands at the top of a stairway leading to the Temple of the Warriors in the city of Chichen Itza, Mexico. Legend says that he emerged from the ocean to create the world, then disappeared back into the sea. In Aztec mythology, he became merged with the powerful god Quetzalcoatl.

CITY BUILDING

Maya civilization was based around numerous individual city-states, each with its own ruler and government. The Maya built their great cities both in the highland and lowland regions of Central America. Each city was carefully planned. At the heart of a city were great plazas, or squares. These were ceremonial areas, surrounded by important religious and government buildings. Such buildings included the large and highly decorated royal palaces, towering pyramid-temples, and ball courts. Groups of temples were linked by enormous stone causeways. Immediately outside the ceremonial center were smaller temples, shrines, and the houses of less important nobles. The ordinary people of the city made their homes outside these sacred areas.

City construction reached its peak during the so-called Maya Classic Period (c. 250–900 C.E.). Many of the major cities, including Tikal, flourished at that time. Later, Chichen Itza in the Yucatan Peninsula of present-day Mexico became the most powerful city. The city's location was chosen because three natural wells provided plentiful water all year round. The city may have flourished until the early thirteenth century, when revolt and civil war led to its decline. Today, Chichen Itza is a World Heritage Site and the most visited of the ancient Maya cities.

Right: This temple stands in the ceremonial center of Tikal in present-day Guatemala. Tikal is the largest of the ancient ruined Maya cities. It reached the height of its power during the Maya Classic Period, but declined and was abandoned in the tenth century.

CREATION OF ANIMALS

The gods set about their task eagerly. They created animals to live in the forests and mountains: deer, birds, pumas, jaguars, and snakes. They gave each of these animals a home to live in where they would be provided with food and shelter.

"Sleep in the fields and valleys by the riverbanks," they told the deer. "And in the thickets and woods."

"You shall live in the trees and among the vines," they told the birds. "There you shall make your nests." Then the gods spoke to the animals. "Hiss, cry, warble, and call as you will, according to your kind," they said. "Speak our names, sing our praises, call on us, and worship us. For we have made you and given you a place to live."

To the gods' dismay, however, the animals were unable to speak. Some of them could squawk or screech, while others could howl, cry, or roar. But they could not

speak words as the gods did. They could not even speak to each other, for each of them made a different sound. The gods were not pleased. If the animals could not speak properly, how could they worship the gods? They had planned for the animals to rule the world.

"Because you cannot speak to us, we have changed our minds," the gods said. "You shall have your food, fields, homes, and nests but we shall make other beings who will honor us. You will become food for each other and for the people to come. This will be your destiny."

Maya Religion

Religion played a central part in Maya life. Like the Aztecs, the Maya worshipped a great many gods and goddesses who, they believed, created and controlled every aspect of the world. The Maya believed that the gods could be helpful or harmful and it was vital to please them in order to obtain their aid.

THE GODS

The Maya's chief god was Itzamna (eet zam-nah), or "Lizard House." He was also known as Hunab Ku (hoo-nahb koo), the creator of the universe. He was considered lord of the heavens. He was credited with teaching the Maya how to write and use their sacred calendar, and with bringing them knowledge of the

Left: This carving shows the god Itzamna holding a snake called a "vision serpent." The snake was associated with spiritual journeys. The Maya believed that people could travel along the snake's body to reach the world of the spirits, or meet the gods hidden in the snake's coils.

Right: The façade of this Maya palace in Sayil, on the Yucatan Peninsula in Mexico, has the face of Chac, the rain god, in the center. In carvings and illustrations, he was shown with a long, spout-like nose for pouring rain onto the Earth. He also had T-shaped eyes, which represented rain falling from the sky.

Left: This reconstruction of a Maya wall painting from Bonampak in Mexico shows a religious ceremony with richly dressed priests and musicians. Religious festivals in honor of the gods took place throughout the year. Priests conducted the festivals and made sacrifices. They also advised the city rulers about important matters.

knowledge of the maize plant. As bringer of writing, he was patron of priests and scribes. He is usually shown as an old man with toothless jaws, sunken cheeks, and a long nose.

Itzamna's wife was called Ix Chel (eesh chel), or "Lady Rainbow." She was goddess of the Moon, healing, and childbirth. Itzamna and Ix Chel had four sons, called the Bacabs. The Bacabs were giants, placed at the four corners of the universe to hold up the sky.

SACRIFICES

Many Maya gods were linked to nature and farming. Because he brought life-giving rain to water the crops, Chac (chahk), the rain god, was one of the most widely worshipped gods. In times of drought, the people of Chichen Itza in Mexico threw offerings into a deep well to win Chac's favor. The offerings consisted of rich treasures and human victims, including children.

Right: The sacred well at Chichen Itza was dedicated to the rain god Chac. Such wells were considered to be entrances to the underworld. Offerings of jade, pottery, and incense were thrown into the well, along with human sacrifices. Excavations have recovered the remains of forty-two individuals, half of them under twenty years old.

PEOPLE OF MUD, WOOD, AND MAIZE

Even though the gods had now created the Earth and the animals, there was still no one to praise and worship them for all that they had achieved. So Gucumatz and Huracan turned their attention to making the first people, who would be obedient and respectful. Their first two attempts at the task were complete failures.

In their first attempt, Gucumatz and Huracan tried to make a person from a lump of mud. But the mud was too soft and slippery, and they could not make the body stick together. It melted away and had no strength. When it tried to walk, it fell into a heap. It could not move its head, and its face was lopsided. It quickly became soaked with water and could not stand up at all. Worse still, although it could speak, the gods could not make any sense of its words. They agreed to break up this body and to start all over again.

PEOPLE OF WOOD

Next, the gods decided to consult an old couple, called Xpiyacoc (shpee-YAH-kok) and Xmucane (shmoo-KAH-nay), to see if human beings could be made out of wood. These two ancient gods, known as Grandfather and Grandmother, had the power to see into the future.

After a silence, the old couple spoke. "Your figures of wood shall come out well," they said. "They shall speak and walk on the Earth."

Gucumatz and Huracan listened carefully to this prophecy. Then, in unison, they said, "Let it be so!"

And with these words, the world was instantly filled with wooden figures. They looked like people, talked like people, and had families and children. The men were made from the wood of the coral tree. The women were made from bulrushes. At first, the gods were pleased with their wooden people, but their joy did not last for long. Even though the people of wood could speak, their faces lacked expression, and their hands and feet had no strength. Their hearts and minds were empty and did not honor the gods who had created and cared for them. Once again, Gucumatz and Huracan had to admit defeat.

Huracan, god of the sky, sent a terrible flood to drown the people of wood, and an army of terrifying demons to break up their bodies. Even the animals in the forests, and the pots and pans in their homes, turned against the wooden people. In all the chaos, the wooden people tried to flee, but there was no escape to be found anywhere. The very few people who managed to survive were turned into monkeys and allowed to live on only in the forests.

Left: A Maya bowl is decorated with figures of quetzal birds. Many Maya works of art were decorated with animal images. The quetzal was linked to the creator god, Gucumatz, also known as the Plumed Serpent. Quetzal feathers were highly prized for making gorgeous costumes for Maya rulers and nobles.

PEOPLE OF MAIZE

The world was still bathed in half-darkness but the gods knew that dawn must come soon. Then the Sun, Moon, and stars would appear in the sky, and the world would be complete. Except that there was one piece of creation still missing—the first human beings. Twice now, Gucumatz and Huracan had tried to create people who would worship them. And twice they had failed. But they were determined to succeed in their task.

Four animals—the parrot, the coyote, the fox, and the crow—brought news of a wonderful place they had found. It was a beautiful land high up in the mountains, known as Bitter Water Place, and it was filled with maize and food of every kind. They showed the gods the way to this place, and Gucumatz and Huracan gave the maize they brought back to Grandmother Xmucane.

Xmucane washed her hands in cold, clear water and ground the maize into flour. She then mixed this flour with the water she had used for washing. From this paste, the gods made the first four men.

This time the gods were very pleased with their work. Unlike their previous creations, the people of maize could talk clearly, and possessed knowledge and understanding. And these new people thanked and praised the gods for making them so perfectly.

"We give you thanks," they said, "two and three times! We have been created, we have been given a mouth and a face, we speak, we think, and we walk. We know what is near and what is far. We give you thanks for having created us!"

But the people of maize also had the power to see far into the future, just like the gods, and the gods became worried. They decided that the people were too much like them, and that they must weaken their powers. They did not want human beings to be the equals of the gods.

So Gucumatz and Huracan took away the people's far-seeing powers. They blew mist into their eyes, clouding their sight, as when a mirror is breathed on. In this way, the people could only see what was close by. Now the gods made four beautiful women to be wives and companions for the four men. And these first men and women were the ancestors of the Maya.

Opposite: This vase painting shows a seated servant girl holding a jug of liquid. Her flattened forehead can be seen clearly, as can her jewelry, which includes earrings and a bracelet, her headdress, and hair ornaments.

WHAT THE MAYA LOOKED LIKE

Illustrations from books and vases show that there were several marks of beauty in Maya times, particularly among the noble classes, which may seem strange to us today. Being cross-eyed was considered very fashionable. To achieve this, mothers hung tiny balls of resin on the hairs falling between their children's eyes. Constant focusing on these made their eyes cross. A flattened forehead was another desirable feature. This was achieved by binding the heads of newborn babies between two boards.

Above: The Maya generally wore simple clothes: loincloths for men and robes for women. Wealthy people could afford jewelry made from precious jade and quetzal feather headdresses. This richly attired figure is clearly a high-ranking Maya noble.

Writing, Counting, and the Calendar

Among many other achievements, the Maya were brilliant communicators and scientists. They were the first people in Central America to develop an advanced form of writing, which was used to keep records of their history, government, and religion. They also made great advances in mathematics and astronomy, developing an accurate yearly calendar.

Right: This detail of a carved wood lintel from one of the temples at Tikal was carved to celebrate a victory over a neighboring city in 743 C.E. The right-hand side shows the face of Tikal's ruler, while the left-hand side shows a series of Maya glyphs.

WRITING

The Maya system of writing used picture symbols, called glyphs. Each symbol represented an object, a combination of sounds, or an idea. A shield and a club, for example, stood for war. Only a very few Maya priests and nobles were able to read and write.

The study of Maya glyphs began in 1827, with the work of the scholar Constantine Rafinesque-Schmaltz (1783–1840), and, by the 1950s, experts had identified the names of gods and animals. They later realized that the glyphs were primarily historical, recording events in the lives of the Maya rulers. The Maya carved glyphs on large stone pillars and slabs, called stelae. These were placed in front of important buildings. Glyphs have also been found painted on walls and vases.

BOOKS

The Maya created books, called codices, from paper made from the fibers of the maguey cactus plant or from fig tree bark. Only four of these books survive, the so-called Madrid, Dresden, Paris, and Grolier codices, which were named by modern scholars. A codex was read from top to bottom, then from left to right.

COUNTING AND THE CALENDAR

Maya mathematicians were highly skilled and devised a system of counting based on the number twenty. Three number symbols—a dot for one, a bar for five, and a shell for zero—could be combined to show all numbers. By studying mathematics and astronomy, the priests developed two kinds of calendars. One was a sacred calendar of 260 days, which was used for predicting auspicious and inauspicious days. The other was a 365-day calendar, divided into eighteen months of twenty days each. This left five days at the end of the year that the Maya regarded as extremely unlucky.

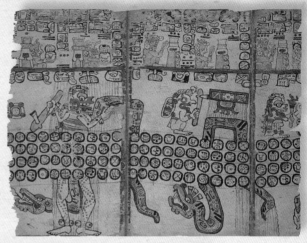

Above: This illustration is from the Madrid Codex, one of the four surviving Mayan codices. It dates from the thirteenth century C.E. and contains information about divination (predicting the future) and rituals for Maya priests.

Below: The ruins of the astronomical observatory still stand at Chichen Itza today. Because of its interior spiral staircase, the building was called El Caracol ("Giant Conch Shell") by the Spanish. The windows in the dome are lined up with the appearance of certain stars at certain dates. From the dome, priests decreed auspicious times for celebrations, rituals, planting maize, and harvesting.

THE HEAVENLY
WEAVING GIRL

The creation of the Earth and people was now complete. But the Earth was still shrouded in darkness. A Sun and Moon were needed in the sky to bring light to the world. But the Sun and Moon lived down on the Earth. The Sun was a handsome young hunter who spent his days searching for deer and other animals in the forests and hills. The Moon was a beautiful girl who worked as a weaver, making cloth in wonderful patterns and colors.

As soon as the Sun set eyes on the Moon, he fell madly in love with her. Every day, he found himself drawn back to her house, where she lived with her grandfather. Every day, he found some excuse to pass by the house in the hope of catching a glimpse of her beautiful face. And now and again, he brought her a fine deer that he had caught in order to show off his strength and hunting skills. The Moon was pleased by the hunter's gifts and by his attention and, very soon, she began to fall in love with him.

THE HUMMINGBIRD SUN

The Moon's grandfather did not approve of the match and did all that he could to stop the love affair going any further. But that did not stop the Sun's wooing of the Moon. He loved her more every day, and he was determined to be with her always.

As well as being brave and strong, the Sun also possessed magical powers. He decided to transform himself into a hummingbird. That way, he could come and go as he pleased without the Moon's grandfather noticing him. He flew among the trees and plants in the grandfather's garden, watching the Moon working away

Mesoamerican Myth

Right: This beautifully crafted pottery figure from Palenque in Mexico is actually an incense burner with a funnel running up the back. On the front is a priest figure who may represent the Sun god. The figure stands on a turtle from which the chief god of the underworld emerges.

busily at her weaving. Then, one day, disaster struck. As the hummingbird hovered by a flower, pretending that it was busy drinking the nectar, the Moon's grandfather accidentally shot it with a clay pellet from a blowgun. Badly wounded, the hummingbird fell to the ground and, immediately, the Sun reverted back to his human form.

When she saw what had happened, the Moon was horrified. She flung aside her weaving and ran to the Sun. Then, keeping his presence a secret from her grandfather, she hid him and nursed him until his wounds had healed. And when the Sun was well again, the Moon ran away with him.

THE GODS' REVENGE
When he found that she was missing, the Moon's grandfather was driven wild with fury.

ARTS AND CRAFTS

Maya craftspeople produced many beautiful works of sculpture and pottery. Artists decorated temple and palace walls with brightly painted figures and scenes from battles and religious festivals. Women were responsible for weaving textiles for making clothes and for paying taxes and tribute to their rulers.

Some of these textiles, especially those woven for rulers and nobles, were richly embroidered. The yarn used was cotton for the ruling classes, and cactus and yucca fibers for ordinary people. The yarn was dyed, and then woven on back-strap looms.

The weaver sat on the ground, with one end of the loom hooked on to a post in the ground, and the other end pulled taut by a strap around the weaver's back. Different colors of yarn were used to give different meanings within the patterns. For example, black represented weapons, yellow symbolized food, and red represented blood. Green was the royal color because it was the color of the quetzal bird's feathers.

Right: This figurine shows a Maya woman weaving on a back-strap loom.

He called upon all the gods to help him find the Sun and Moon, and to stop them from running away.

From their home high above the Earth, the gods could see far and wide and it was impossible to hide from them for long. They began their search for the Sun and the Moon, scouring every possible hiding place. Finally the gods spotted the fugitive couple paddling in a canoe on a river far below. The rain god picked up a thunderbolt and hurled it straight at the pair. At once, the Sun changed himself into a turtle and began to swim away. Then he turned the Moon into a crab, but it was too late to save her.

The Moon was broken into pieces, and died soon afterward. Heartbroken, the Sun collected up the Moon's remains with great care and gentleness. Then, with the help of a band of glittering, jewel-like dragonflies, he placed the pieces of the Moon's body inside thirteen hollow logs and sealed the logs shut.

The Sun waited for thirteen days, then, one by one, he opened up the logs again and peered inside. The first twelve logs were filled with poisonous snakes and stinging insects which slithered and flew off into the world and have been a nuisance to people ever since. But, when the Sun opened the thirteenth log, he could not believe his eyes. Inside, he found the Moon, miraculously brought back to life!

RISING INTO THE SKY

The Sun and Moon were reunited despite the gods' best efforts to keep them apart. For many more years, they continued to live happily down on Earth. But the Moon was homesick and had been regularly returning to her grandfather's house to visit him. The Sun found out about her secret visits and determined to put an end to them.

The Sun was afraid that the Moon would leave him for ever, so he carried her off to exile in the sky. There the Sun and Moon shine to this day and until the end of the world.

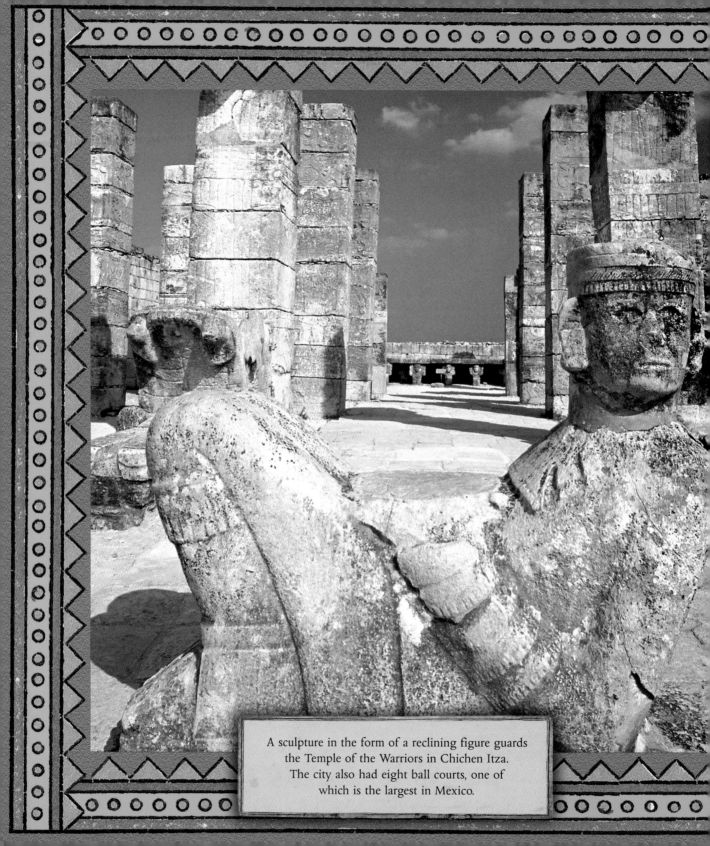

A sculpture in the form of a reclining figure guards
the Temple of the Warriors in Chichen Itza.
The city also had eight ball courts, one of
which is the largest in Mexico.

TALES OF THE HERO TWINS

In Maya mythology, there are a great many stories about a pair of twin gods, called Xbalanque (shi-bah-LAN-kay) and Hunahpu (hoo-NAH-poo), who were known as the Hero Twins. Among their many exploits, they fought the monstrous Seven Macaw to make the Earth safe and had adventures in the underworld.

The Hero Twins' father, Hun Hunahpu (hoon hoo-NAH-poo), died before the Twins were born. Following defeat in a ball game, Hun Hunahpu had been killed by the lords of the underworld and his skull had been hung on the branch of a tree. When the daughter of one of the lords approached the tree, the skull started speaking to her. Shortly afterward, she became pregnant with the Hero Twins and had to flee from her father's fury to live on the surface of the Earth. The Hero Twins grew up to avenge their father's death, and they used their cunning and trickery to defeat the lords of the underworld.

THE HERO TWINS AND
THE SEVEN MACAW

After the flood that destroyed the people of wood, the Earth was covered in cloudy twilight. The faces of the Sun and Moon were hidden. A huge number of monstrous beings lived on the Earth and were intent on destroying it. The greatest of these was a monster bird called the Seven Macaw, who had two sons. It was left to the Hero Twins to rid the world of the Seven Macaw and his sons, and to make the Earth and sky safe.

In the time after the great flood, a terrible bird called the Seven Macaw lived in a splendid nest made from silver. He liked to sit in his nest, high above the Earth, preening his shimmering feathers. Seven Macaw was very proud of his feathers and riches.

"Great is my glory and splendor," he boasted. "My eyes are ringed with silver and shine like emeralds. My teeth are encrusted with jewels. My nose shines like the Moon. The face of the Earth lights up whenever I pass by. So, then, I am the Sun and the Moon— the greatest god of all!"

Angered by the Seven Macaw's endless boasting and false claims, the Hero Twins— Hunahpu and Xbalanque—decided to teach him a lesson. They were both skilled and cunning hunters, well practiced at shooting animals and birds with their blowpipes. One morning, they hid underneath Seven Macaw's favorite tree, where he liked to come each day to feed on the succulent fruit. As Seven Macaw was eating, Hunahpu picked up his blowpipe, took aim, and fired straight at the bird, striking him on the jaw. Screaming in pain, Seven Macaw fell straight out of the tree. Quickly, Hunahpu ran over to overpower him, but Seven Macaw grabbed Hunahpu's arm and wrenched it clean off. Carrying Hunahpu's arm in his beak, Seven Macaw made his painful way home. There, he complained bitterly to his wife about his broken jaw, which had given him a terrible toothache. He hung Hunahpu's arm above the fire and declared that, if the Twins wanted it back, they would have to come and get it.

THE TWINS PLAY A TRICK

Having thought long and hard, the Hero Twins devised another plan to outwit Seven Macaw. They went to see a wise old couple, called Great White Peccary and Great White Tapir.

"Come with us to the house of Seven Macaw," the Twins said. "We will follow you and you can tell him that we are your grandchildren. You can pretend to be healers with a cure for his toothache. He is in such pain that he will accept any help gratefully. Then, when his guard is down, we'll get the arm back."

"Very well," answered the old man and woman.

The Twins' plan worked perfectly. When they reached Seven Macaw's house, they found him screaming in pain because of his injury. He could not eat or sleep.

The old couple told Seven Macaw that the only way to cure his toothache was to replace his old jeweled teeth with new teeth made from finely ground bone. But the teeth they put in his mouth were nothing more than grains of corn. Instantly, his face began to sag and he did not look like a lord anymore. Then, while he was under their power, the couple took away the shining circles of silver around Seven Macaw's eyes.

Right: A detail from a Maya painted vase shows one of the Hero Twins hunting waterbirds with his blowgun. Legend says that, from an early age, the Hero Twins were skilled hunters, catching birds and other animals for food.

Tales of the Hero Twins 73

SACRED ANIMALS

In Maya and other Mesoamerican cultures, animals played a very important part both in everyday life and in religion. Many works of art were decorated with the animals that the Maya saw in the forests and hills around them, such as jaguars, quetzals, monkeys, and snakes. Many of the Maya gods appeared in animal form. The Plumed Serpent, Gucumatz, was linked with the quetzal bird, associated with wise leadership. At night, the Maya believed that the Sun god was reborn as a mighty jaguar who traveled through the underworld to do battle with the lords of the dead. The jaguar was feared and admired as a great hunter, and the Hero Twins are often shown with spotted skins to show their hunting prowess.

Below: The Maya believed that Seven Macaw's likeness could be seen on Earth in the scarlet macaw. These striking birds are found in the rain forests of Central and South America. The scarlet macaw's strangely shaped beak suggests a damaged jaw, and the featherless patches around its eyes show where its silver circles were stripped away.

Stripped of his splendor and riches, of which he had been so proud, Seven Macaw grew weaker and weaker until he died. Then it was easy for the Hero Twins to remove Hunahpu's severed arm from above the fireplace. All that was left was for the old couple to put the arm carefully back in place so that it healed perfectly.

SEVEN MACAW'S SONS

With Seven Macaw gone, the Hero Twins turned their attention to his two sons, who were just as vain and boastful as their father. One was a giant called Zipacna (see-POK-nah), the Earth Crocodile, who claimed to have created all the mountains on Earth. Seven Macaw's second son was called Earthquake, and his boast was that, with a simple tap of his foot, he could make the mountains shake and crash down.

Zipacna's favorite foods were crabs and fish, which he hunted from the riverbank. To trick Zipacna, the Hero Twins built a huge false crab from leaves, with a stone for its shell. They hid the crab at the bottom of a deep ravine at the foot of a large mountain, then went to find Zipacna. He had not caught any food that day and was hungry. The Twins told him about the crab, and took him off to find it. Down the slippery rock face Zipacna went, and reached deep into the ravine. But, just as he was about to grab the crab, the Twins slid the mountain on top of him and he was turned into stone.

Next, the Hero Twins set off to find Earthquake. When they found him, they pretended to be simple hunters from the mountains. They told Earthquake about a large mountain they had seen in the east, so high that it looked over the tops of all the other hills. Now Earthquake had not seen this mountain, or he would have demolished it. The Twins offered to lead him to the mountain, where he would be able to show off his powers to them.

On the way, the Twins shot some birds and stopped to roast them on a fire. Unbeknown to Earthquake, Hunahpu and Xbalanque put a spell on the birds as they cooked. Soon the birds were ready and Earthquake's mouth began to water. He ate his share of the food greedily, before the three travelers set off once more. But already Earthquake's strength was fading.

When they finally reached the mountain, Earthquake's legs had become so weak that he could not even tap his foot. However hard he tried, the mountain stayed standing. The Twins' magic spell had worked. His powers gone, Earthquake could not prevent the Twins from grabbing him and tying him up. They buried his body in the ground, so that he could hold up the mountains instead of destroying them.

THE HERO TWINS AND
THE MAIZE FIELD

When the Twins' pregnant mother left the underworld, she made her way to their grandmother's house. Soon afterward, the Twins were born in the nearby woods. Their mother took them back to their grandmother's, but they cried so loudly at night that their grandmother banished them from the house. Their mother made them a bed on an anthill nearby, and then in some thistles, where they slept peacefully.

The Hero Twins grew up alongside their two elder brothers, who were their grandmother's favorites. The brothers, Hunbatz (hoon-bahts) and Hunchouen (hoon-tchoo-ayn), knew that the Twins were destined for greatness and were wildly jealous of them. They treated the younger boys very badly and gave them little to eat.

So, one day, Hunahpu and Xbalanque took their elder brothers hunting with them and tricked them into climbing a tree to fetch the birds they had shot with their blowpipes. While their unkind brothers were up the tree, the Twins turned them into monkeys, who were sent to live in the forest.

GARDENING SKILLS

With her favorite grandsons gone, the Twins worked hard to win their grandmother's love. They decided to start by clearing and planting the maize field that their brothers had once kept.

They picked up their axes, picks, and hoes and set off into the forest. As they left the house, they spoke to their grandmother:

"Dear Grandmother," they said, "would you kindly come to the field at midday and bring our food? We will be hungry after all our hard work."

"Very well, my grandsons," the old woman replied.

But the Hero Twins had no intention of doing any work at all. When they reached the field, they simply stuck their tools in the ground and watched as the tools set to work by themselves. The picks and hoes dug the soil, picking out thistles and brambles. The axe chopped down trees and vines, one after the other. Before very long, the tools had cleared the whole of the field.

While the Twins waited for the tools to finish, they practiced shooting with their blowpipes. To be on the safe side, they asked a dove to call out to them when it saw their grandmother arrive with their food. A little while later, the dove gave a long, low coo. The Twins leaped into action. They put down their blowpipes, grabbed some tools, and rubbed dirt on their faces and hands to make it look as if they had been busy.

Left: This bowl is decorated with a deer. It was found in Peten in modern-day Guatemala, and dates from c. 600 to 900 C.E., when the Maya produced some of their greatest ceramics. The deer was an important source of food for the Maya, and the Hero Twins were sometimes portrayed as deer hunters.

Their grandmother was very impressed with their hard work and gave them a fine lunch, which they ate at once.

When they returned home that evening, the Twins pretended to be exhausted by their toil. They complained about the blisters on their hands and their aching arms and legs. But their plan was about to backfire.

A DIFFERENT DESTINY

When the Twins returned to the maize field the following day, they got a nasty shock. They found that the trees and vines were standing again, and the brambles and thistles had grown back. So they set their tools to work again, and soon a new plot was cleared.

"Who could have played this trick on us?" the Twins wondered. "No doubt it was the animals. We'll have to stay overnight and catch them if they come again."

So the Twins hid themselves behind a tree and waited for darkness to fall. As they watched, the animals—the puma, the jaguar, the deer, the rabbit, the fox, the coyote, the peccary, and the rat—came wandering into the field. "Rise up, trees! Rise up, vines! Rise up and grow tall!" they sang.

The Twins dashed out from their hiding place and tried to catch the animals. The puma and the jaguar were much too fast for the boys, and vanished into the moonlight. The deer and the rabbit came within grasping distance, but they, too, got away. As did the fox, the coyote, and the peccary.

The Twins were furious. But at last they managed to chase down the rat. They held him over the fire to make him talk.

The rat told them that it was not their business to plant maize: their destiny lay elsewhere. They must follow their father and uncle into the underworld and defeat the lords of death who ruled there. But first they must find the ring, the gloves, and the ball that their father and uncle had used to play the ball game. These were hanging from the roof in their grandmother's house, where she had hidden them.

Next morning, when they got home, the Twins distracted their grandmother's attention while the rat climbed up into the roof and began to gnaw through the rope that held the ball.

The Twins sent the old lady out for food, then for water, then for more food. Finally, the ring, gloves, and ball were all found. The Twins took them and ran quickly to hide them on the road that led to the ball court.

GODS OF MAIZE

Maize was the Maya's most important crop and their staple source of food. It was ground into flour for making bread and was also used to make an alcoholic drink. So vital was maize to the Maya's existence that Yum Caax (yum kah-ash), the god of agriculture and of maize in particular, was a deity of exceptional importance. He was always shown as a young man, sometimes with an ear of maize in his headdress. Like the maize with which he was associated, Yum Caax had many enemies and his fate was controlled by the gods of wind, rain, drought, and famine. Another maize god, known as the "Young Maize God," is often portrayed on Maya vases along with his identical twin. These two gods have been identified by scholars as the father and uncle of the Hero Twins.

Left: This funerary mask, dating from c. 200 to 600 C.E., depicts the supremely important Maya maize god.

The Sacred Ball Game

As well as being a fast and furious sport, the ball game was sacred to the Maya. It had its roots in the divine struggle of good and evil between the Hero Twins and the lords of the underworld. To the Maya, the ball court represented the Earth, and the ball stood for the Sun and the Moon.

No one knows exactly how the ball game was played, but it must have been an exciting and dangerous spectacle.

Right: This stele shows a priest dressed as a ball player making offerings to the gods.

RULES OF THE GAME

Two teams of eleven players tried to hit a rubber ball through a small stone hoop high off the ground. They had to keep the ball in play using parts of their body, such as their hips, knees, thighs, and forearms. Players were not allowed to use their hands or feet. The game was made more difficult by the fact that the ball was made from solid rubber, so it was hard and heavy.

Above: This Maya stone figurine depicts a ball player dressed in the ball game costume. Players entered the court dressed in the finest animal skins, jewelry, and feather headdresses. For the game itself, they probably wore little more than protective gear to lessen the injuries caused by the hard ball. This included padded hip, knee, and forearm protectors made from animal hide, a hide or wooden yoke around the waist, and sometimes a helmet.

Right: The Great Ball Court in the city of Chichen Itza was shaped like a capital "I." The playing alley had tall stone sides so that players could bank the ball to keep it in play. Spectators would watch from benches along the sides. Courts were decorated with carvings of ball games and sacrifices. The average size of a ball court was about 120 x 30 feet (36 x 9 m), but the Great Ball Court was much larger at 600 x 230 feet (185 x 70 m).

Serious injuries were commonplace as players attempted to keep the ball in motion. If a team managed to get the ball through a hoop, they were immediately declared the winners. It seems likely, however, that games often ended in a tie. Winners were showered with praise and prizes, such as gold and turquoise jewelry, feathers, slaves, and lands. In some cases, the losers were sacrificed to the gods, and their heads put on display.

Left: This ball court ring is from the Great Ball Court at Chichen Itza. Two stone rings jutted out from the opposing walls of the playing alley, about 27 feet (8 m) from the ground. They were decorated with carvings of animals and plants. Each ring had a hole in the middle just wide enough to fit a ball through.

THE HERO TWINS
IN THE UNDERWORLD

Having found the ring, gloves, and ball that had belonged to their father, the Hero Twins were at last ready to fulfill their destiny and avenge their father's death. They went to play ball on their father's favorite ball court on the far eastern edge of the Earth. They played happily for many hours, until, as with their father and uncle before them, the ball court became the path they used to descend into Xibalba (shee-BAHL-bah), the underworld.

As the Hero Twins played the ball game, the pounding of the ball made the ground shake. The shuddering reached right through the ground to Xibalba, where it disturbed the lords of the underworld, particularly One Death and Seven Death—just as had happened with the Hero Twins' ill-fated father and uncle. One Death and Seven Death sent their owl messengers to summon the Twins to the underworld so that they could challenge them to a ball game. The owls followed the path straight to the Hero Twins' house and gave the message to their grandmother.

"Tell them to come without fail, within seven days," said the owls. "The lords will be waiting for them."

Their grandmother was very worried. She did not want her grandsons to follow in her sons' footsteps. They, too, had been summoned to the underworld to play a ball game, and they had never returned. But she did not dare to disobey the lords of the underworld. She gave the message to a louse and sent it to fetch the Twins. On the way, it was swallowed by a toad who, in turn, was swallowed by a snake. The snake continued along the road to the ball court, until it was swallowed by a hawk, who flew to the ball court and perched on one corner, near where the Twins were still playing.

Right: A Maya vase is decorated with a scene showing the Hero Twins in conversation with the god Itzamna. Itzamna is pointing toward a large basket on top of which sits a skull and some jewelry and clothing. These probably belonged to the Twins' dead father.

When the Twins heard the hawk's cawing cry, they dropped the ball, seized their blowguns, and shot the hawk in the eye.

"What is your business here?" they asked the hawk, as it lay on the ground.

"Heal my injured eye and I will tell you," the hawk replied.

So the Twins picked some rubber off their ball and used it to mend the bird's eye. And that is why the hawk's eyes are circled with black.

"Now speak," the Twins told the hawk.

So the hawk spat out the snake, and the snake spat out the toad. Finally, the Twins found the louse, stuck to the toad's teeth. And the louse delivered its sinister message.

THE JOURNEY TO XIBALBA

The Twins ran home quickly. They said goodbye to their weeping grandmother and set off to Xibalba. It was a terrifying journey. First, they descended a steep cliff face, then they had to cross rivers of corruption and blood. Then they paused at a crossroads. They decided to send a mosquito ahead to gather information.

"Bite the lords of the underworld, one by one," they told it, "and your reward will be to suck the blood of travelers for evermore."

THE TOMB OF KING PACAL

Noble and wealthy Maya were buried in elaborate tombs, surrounded by precious goods. One of the richest Maya tombs was discovered by archaeologists in 1949. While excavating the ruins of the Temple of the Inscriptions at Palenque, they found a staircase leading deep down inside the pyramid. It led to the tomb of Pacal the Great (603–683 C.E.), a ruler of the city. Nothing remained of the robes in which he had been buried, but the fabulous jewelry that had adorned his body was still in place. Most spectacular of all was his exquisite death mask, made from more than 200 pieces of jade. But the most stunning object in the tomb was the richly carved coffin lid. It showed Pacal falling, like the Sun at sunset, into Xibalba, ready to do battle with the lords of the underworld.

Below: This engraving of Pacal the Great, ruler of Palenque, shows him with a pipe in his hand. He ascended the throne at the age of twelve and lived to the great age of eighty.

So the mosquito bit the underworld lords and bothered them so much that the lords called out to each other by name. When the Twins finally met the lords, they were able to greet them by name, which unsettled the lords even more.

Straight away on their arrival, One Death and Seven Death tried to trick the Twins into sitting on a seat of red-hot stones, but the Twins refused. Furious, the lords led the Twins into the House of Gloom. They gave them two lighted cigars and two burning torches to light up the darkness. But they told the Twins to return the cigars and torches unchanged in the morning, which meant that they could not let them burn down at all.

Yet again, the Twins were equal to the test. All night, they let the cigars and the torches burn away. And then, in the morning, in place of the flames, they attached red macaw feathers to the torches and fireflies to the cigars, so that they appeared to have been freshly lit.

THE FIRST BALL GAME

The underworld lords were worried now. These visitors seemed more troublesome than any who had come down from Earth before. Determined to defeat them, the lords challenged the Twins to a ball game.

They insisted that the Twins use the lords' own ball, which was no more than a human skull. As soon as the game began, the lords threw the ball straight at the Twins. The skull burst open and a sharp dagger came shooting out. It danced and dodged around the ball court, seeking to kill the Twins. But the Twins managed to outrun it, jumping and weaving to escape its blade.

The Twins then insisted on playing with their own ball—but they allowed themselves to be beaten. They knew that this was not the moment to claim victory. There were many more trials still to overcome.

THE HOUSE OF KNIVES

Surprised by the Twins' defeat, the lords of the underworld claimed their prize for the ball game. As the winners, they demanded four gourds of flowers that the Twins must gather and bring to them early the next morning. To make the Twins' task more difficult, the lords threw them into the hideous House of Knives.

Locked in their cell, it seemed impossible that the Twins would find any flowers for the lords. There was no way out of this terrible place. Besides, their lives were in grave danger, for the air was filled with flying, razor-sharp knives. The lords hoped that the Twins would die there—they were becoming far too troublesome.

Right: This stone urn shows the face of a bat, an animal believed to torment travelers in Xibalba. One of the houses that travelers had to brave was filled with screeching bats. It is in the House of Bats that Hunahpu had his head torn off.

But the Twins were not easily killed. They spoke to the knives and asked them to be still, promising them the meat of animals to cut. And immediately the knives were still. Then the Twins turned their attention to finding flowers for the lords. During the night, they summoned the ants that lived in the underworld and sent them to collect flowers from the lords' own gardens. Guessing that the Twins might try to raid the gardens, the lords had set birds to guard them. But the birds did not notice the tiny ants cutting flowers to fill four gourds. Next morning, Hunahpu and Xbalanque took the flowers to the underworld lords. It was obvious where the flowers had come from. Once more, the lords were furious.

THE FIVE HOUSES

Determined to get the better of the Twins, the lords sent them to spend the next night in the freezing House of Cold. But still the Twins did not die. Somehow, they conjured up some logs to make a fire and, to the lords' amazement, were still alive in the morning.

Next the Twins were sent into the House of Jaguars in the hope that they would be torn to death. Still the Twins did not die. They tamed the snarling animals by throwing them some bones. The following night, the lords threw the Twins into the House of

Fire—but, of course, they were not even burned. To the lords' astonishment and despair, the Twins emerged in the morning safe and sound.

The next trial was the House of Bats, which was full of shrieking vampire bats. Here the Twins slept inside their blowpipes so that they did not get bitten. Having waited there for many hours, however, Hunahpu became impatient. He poked his head out of his blowpipe to see if the day had dawned yet. At that very moment, a giant bat came flying past and snatched off Hunahpu's head. The bat carried it to the underworld ball court, where the lords of death rejoiced. At last, the lords had won a victory over the Hero Twins! They decided to challenge the Twins to another ball game.

Immediately, Xbalanque called on all of the animals to bring their food to him. Some brought rotten things, while others brought leaves and grass. Finally, the coati arrived carrying a large squash. Xbalanque used the squash to make a new head for Hunahpu, and the two set off for the ball court.

THE FINAL BALL GAME

The lords of the underworld began the game by throwing in Hunahpu's real head as the ball. The first time Xbalanque touched it, he struck it so hard that it bounced out of the ball court and into the nearby oak wood. The Twins had previously ordered a rabbit to hide among the trees, and now it came leaping out to cause a distraction.

THE MAYA UNDERWORLD

In Maya mythology, the underworld was called Xibalba, or the "Place of Fright." It was described in the *Popol Vuh* as a dark, dismal city or region beneath the Earth, which was ruled by twelve gods of death, known as the Lords of Xibalba. The most powerful were Lords One Death and Seven Death. The remaining ten lords were demons with chilling names, such as Jaundice Demon, Skull Scepter, Blood Gatherer, and Lord of Stabbing. Each presided over various forms of human sufferings, such as sickness, starvation, fear, and pain. Like the Aztecs, the Maya believed that the road to Xibalba was filled with obstacles for the souls of the dead. Once in Xibalba, more terrors awaited in the six deadly houses: the Houses of Gloom, Knives, Cold, Jaguars, Fire, and Bats.

Mesoamerican Myth

Confused, the lords chased right after it, thinking that it was the ball. Meanwhile, Xbalanque retrieved Hunahpu's real head and switched it for the squash.

When the lords returned, the game began again, this time using the squash as the ball. But, after a couple of strikes, the squash began to split and its seeds came spilling out. Once again, the lords had been outwitted by the Twins.

VICTORY OVER THE UNDERWORLD

Although the Twins had been victorious, they knew that the underworld lords would not rest until they were dead. Shortly afterward, the lords invited the Twins to a great feast at which a huge bonfire was burning. The lords dared the Twins to leap over the fire. But, realizing that the lords only wanted their death, the Twins bravely jumped into the fire and were burned alive.

The lords of Xibalba were filled with joy. They whistled and shouted. "At last, we have overcome them! They have given themselves up!" they exclaimed.

The lords then ground up the Twins' charred bones and threw them into the river. But instead of drifting away, the bones settled on the bottom—and, five days later, the Twins appeared as two large fish. The very next day, they returned to Xibalba, disguised as poor, traveling performers and dressed in rags.

The lords of Xibalba heard of the wonderful dances of the two unknown performers and summoned them to perform at their palace. After their dances, the Twins performed several magic tricks. First, they sacrificed a dog and brought it back to life. Then they burned the lords' palace down before making it whole again. Next, Xbalanque cut Hunahpu's head off, only to put it back in place again. The lords of death were delighted by the spectacle. They begged the Twins to do the same to them. This time, however, the lords were sacrificed for real. The Twins killed One Death, then Seven Death, and did not bring either of them back to life. All the other Xibalbans fled.

And so, through cunning and trickery, the Hero Twins conquered the evil underworld. But before they left Xibalba, there was just one more task to complete. They found the remains of their father and uncle, and put their bodies back together. They told them that they must stay in Xibalba, but they would always be honored. Then Xbalanque and Hunahpu rose into the sky, where they became the Sun and the Moon.

Opposite: A terracotta relief of the Maya sun god was found on a pyramid wall in Campeche in Mexico. In the *Popol Vuh*, the Hero Twins rise into the sky to become the Sun and the Moon.

TIMELINE OF THE AZTEC AND MAYA

c. 1800 B.C.E.–250 C.E.
The so-called Maya Preclassic Period is at its peak. During this period, agriculture spreads, the population grows, and larger settlements appear. By the end of the period, major public construction projects have been erected.

c. 1200–400 B.C.E.
The Olmec civilization flourishes in the lowlands of south-central Mexico. This may be the first civilization in the Western Hemisphere to develop a writing system.

c. 1000 B.C.E.
The first Maya farmers may have settled in small villages in the region of El Peten in the lowlands of northern Guatemala.

c. 600–400 B.C.E.
The Maya build their first large temple-pyramids.

c. 400 B.C.E.–650 C.E.
The great city of Monte Alban in southern Mexico flourishes. It is the center of the Zapotec civilization and features step-pyramids, temples, tombs, and a court for playing the ball game.

c. 200–300 B.C.E.
The earliest inscriptions are made in Maya script.

c. 250–900 C.E.
The Maya Classic Period is at its peak. Maya culture is centered in the lowland rain forests of Guatemala. The Maya found their greatest cities, including Tikal in Guatemala and Copan in Honduras. They also make amazing advances in the arts and sciences, and put up stelae to record important events.

c. 550–900 C.E.
The Maya settle the city of Chichen Itza, the ruins of which still stand in the Yucatan Peninsula in present-day Mexico.

615–683 C.E.
Pacal the Great reigns in the great Maya city of Palenque. His elaborate tomb is rediscovered in 1949.

c. 700–900 C.E.
Maya culture goes into decline as many lowland cities are abandoned. A combination of overpopulation, disease, crop failures, and war may be to blame.

c. 900 C.E.
The Maya Postclassic Period begins. The lowland cities have been abandoned, and new cities are built in the Yucatan, Mexico, and in the Guatemalan highlands. Chichen Itza in Yucatan becomes the most powerful city.

c. 900–1187 C.E.
The Toltec civilization flourishes in central Mexico, based around the city known to the Aztecs as Tollan.

c. 1200–1300
The Aztecs make their 100-year-long migration south from Aztlan (which may be a real or a mythical region) to the Valley of Mexico.

c. 1248

The Aztecs settle in Chapultepec, a hill on the shores of Lake Texcoco.

c. 1299

The Aztecs are ousted from Chapultepec and the ruler of Culhuacan gives them permission to settle in his territory.

1323

The Aztecs ask the ruler of Culhuacan for his daughter and then sacrifice her to the gods. They are immediately expelled.

1325

Forced to flee, the Aztecs make their way to a small island in Lake Texcoco and begin to build their city of Tenochtitlan, which will eventually be home to 200,000 people.

1376

The Aztecs elect their first emperor, Acamapichtli, who reigns until 1395.

1428

The Aztec Triple Alliance is formed from three cities: Tenochtitlan, Texcoco, and Tlacopan. The alliance continues to rule the area around the Valley of Mexico until the Spanish conquest a century later.

1428–1440

Itzcoatl, the first emperor of the Triple Alliance, begins expanding the alliance's territory toward the south.

1440–1469

Moctezuma I reigns as the Aztec emperor, continuing to expand it. During his reign, Huitzilopochtli becomes the most important of the Aztec gods.

1473

The Aztecs of Tenochtitlan conquer neighboring Tlatelolco and unite the two cities.

c. 1502–1520

Moctezuma II reigns as the Aztec emperor. When he comes to the throne, the Aztec Empire is at the height of its powers and at its greatest extent.

1519

The Spanish, led by Hernando Cortés, arrive in Mexico. Cortés reaches the Aztec capital of Tenochtitlan in November.

1520

Moctezuma is killed while in the custody of the Spanish, possibly by a rock thrown by one of his own people.

1521

The Spanish lay siege to Tenochtitlan and the city finally falls. In August, the last Aztec emperor, Cuauhtemoc, surrenders to Cortés.

1697

The Spanish finally conquer all the Maya lands when the last Maya state of Tayasal is subdued.

GLOSSARY

archaeologist A person who studies human cultures of the past through the analysis of architecture, artifacts, and other remains.

Aztlan The "Land of the Cranes." The place where the Aztecs originated, which may have been located in the far north of Mexico, or may have been a mythical place.

ball game A fast and furious game played by the Aztecs and Maya, which had important religious significance.

causeway A large bridge built over water and used as roads. Three huge causeways linked Tenochtitlan to the mainland.

Chac The Maya god of rain.

Chalchiuhtlicue The Aztec goddess of oceans, rivers, and the east.

chinampa Island created by the Aztecs in Lake Texcoco for growing crops.

Coatlicue An Aztec earth goddess and mother of Huitzilopochtli.

codex (plural: **codices**) Concertina-style book produced by the Aztecs and Maya before and after the Spanish conquest. Also called a painted book.

glyph Stylized picture symbols used by the Aztecs and Maya instead of letters to represent words, objects, and ideas.

Gucumatz The Maya sea god who, along with Huracan, created the world.

Hero Twins In Maya mythology, twin gods who defeat the lords of the Underworld and become the Sun and the Moon.

Huitzilopochtli The Aztec god of the Sun and of war, who led the Aztecs to Tenochitlan.

Hunahpu In Maya mythology, one of the Hero Twins.

Huracan The Maya sky god who, along with Gucumatz, created the world.

Itzamna The chief god of the Maya, lord of the heavens, day, and night.

Ix Chel The wife of Itzamna and the Maya goddess of the moon.

Mesoamerica The region inhabited by the Aztecs and Maya, from central Mexico south to the northern part of Central America.

Mictlan The Aztec underworld.

Mictlantechuhtli The Aztec god of the dead, and Lord of Mictlan.

Nanahuatzin The Aztec god who became the Fifth Sun.

Ometeotl The supreme creator god of the Aztecs.

Popol Vuh The "Book of the Community" of the Quiche Maya of Guatemala which begins with the Maya creation myth, followed by stories of the Hero Twins.

quetzal A rain forest bird prized in Mesoamerica for its beautiful feathers.

Quetzalcoatl The Aztec god of the wind and of the west.

stele (plural: **stelae**) Large stone slab erected by the Maya and inscribed with details of wars and other events in their rulers' lives.

Tecuciztecatl The Aztec god who became the Moon, during the Fifth Sun.

Tenochtitlan The capital city of the Aztec Empire, built on an island in Lake Texcoco in 1325, the site of present-day Mexico City.

Teotihuacan An ancient city about 25 miles (40 km) to the northeast of Tenochitlan.

Texcoco, Lake A lake in Mexico which used to cover a large area in the Valley of Mexico. The lake was drained after the Spanish conquest.

Tezcatlipoca The Aztec god of the night and of the north.

Tlaloc The Aztec god of rain and fertility, and of the south.

Tollan The glittering capital of the Toltec civilization. It is also known as Tula.

Toltec The name of the warlike civilization that dominated Mesoamerica from about 900 to 1200 C.E.

tribute Taxes in the form of crops and goods that were paid by conquered towns and cities to the Aztec emperor.

Xbalanque In Maya mythology, one of the Hero Twins.

Xibalba The Maya underworld.

Xipe Totec The Aztec god of springtime and new growth.

Xiuhtechuhtli The Aztec god of fire, who ruled the Fifth Sun.

Xochiquetzal The Aztec goddess of the earth, love, beauty, and weaving.

Yum Caax The Maya god of agriculture, and particularly of maize.

FOR MORE INFORMATION

BOOKS

The following is a selection of books that have been used in the making of this volume, plus recommendations for further reading.

Bacquedano, Elizabeth. *Eyewitness Guides: Aztec.*
  London: Dorling Kindersley, 1993.
Coe, Michael D. *The Maya (Sixth Edition).* London: Thames & Hudson, 2002.
Drew, David. *The Lost Chronicles of the Maya Kings.*
  London: Phoenix Press, 2004.
Jones, David M. and Phillips, Charles. *The Aztec and Maya World: Everyday Life, Society and Culture in Ancient Central America and Mexico.* London: Lorenz Books, 2006.
Longhena, Maria. *Ancient Mexico, History and Culture of the Maya, Aztecs and Other Pre-Columbian Populations.* Vercelli: White Star, 2006.
Lost Civilizations: Aztecs: Reign of Blood and Splendour.
  New York: Time-Life Books, 1992.
Matos Moctezuma, Eduardo. *The Great Temple of the Aztecs.*
  London: Thames & Hudson, 1994.
Pasztory, Esther. *Aztec Art.* New York: Harry N. Abrams, 1983.
Phillips, Charles. *The Mythology of the Aztec and Maya.*
  London: Anness Publishing, 2006.
Shearer, Robert J. *The Ancient Maya (Fifth Edition).*
  Stanford: Stanford University Press, 1994.
Taube, Karl. *The Legendary Past: Aztec and Maya Myths.*
  London: British Museum Press, 1993.
Tedlock, Dennis. *Popol Vuh.* London: Simon & Schuster, 1996.
Townsend, Richard F. *The Aztecs.* London: Thames & Hudson, 1993.
Willis, Roy, ed. *World Mythology: The Illustrated Guide.* London: Simon & Schuster, 1993.

WEB SITES

www.ancientmexico.com
An educational site focusing on ancient Mexico, featuring maps and original sources, including a letter from Cortés to Charles V describing his meeting with the Aztec emperor.

www.latinamericanstudies.org/aztecs
Information about the Aztec Empire, culture, and religion, together with details of codices and other archaeological evidence.

www.azteccalendar.com
An introduction to the complexities of the Aztec calendar, with dates written out in Aztec script.

www.sacred-texts.com/nam/maya/pvgm
An adaptation by Delia Goetz and Sylvanus Griswold Morley of a translation of the Maya *Popol Vuh* by Adrian Recino.

www.ballgame.org
A helpful site giving the history of the Maya sacred ball game, its rules, and its religious and cultural importance.

www.maya-archaeology.org
Information about Maya art, architecture, religion, and writing, with details of the latest excavations and archaeological finds.

MUSEUMS

The British Museum, London
www.thebritishmuseum.ac.uk
A fantastic collection of Aztec and Maya artifacts, including codices and sculptures.

National Museum of Anthropology, Mexico City
www.mexicocity.com.mx
The collection of the major archaeological finds gathered in Mexico since the eighteenth century.

Museo del Templo Mayor, Mexico City
www.archaeology.la.asu.edu
Located in the archaeological district of Mexico City, the museum has eight halls displaying material excavated from the site of the Great Temple of Tenochitlan.

Museo Popol Vuh, Guatemala City
www.popolvuh.ufm.edu.gt
An important collection of Maya art and artifacts, including displays of animals in Maya art.

Copan Museum, Copan, Honduras
www.maya-archaeology.org/museums/copan/copan.html
Art and artifacts from Copan, including a virtual reality tour of the ball court.

INDEX

ACKNOWLEDGMENTS

Sources: AA = Art Archive   WFA = Werner Forman Archive
BAL = Bridgeman Art Library

b = bottom c = center t = top l = left r = right

Front cover: top Art Archive; bottom Corbis/Ulises Ruiz/EPA
Back cover: top Bridgeman Art Library; bottom Werner Forman Archive

Pages: 1 Corbis/Alison Wright; 2–3 Corbis/Jan Butchofsky-Houser; 7 WFA/British Museum, London; 10 Corbis/Jose Fuste Raga; 13 WFA/ National Museum of Anthropology, Mexico; 15 WFA/British Museum; 16 WFA/Liverpool Museum; 18t AA/National Archives Mexico/Mireille Vautier; 18b WFA/Museum Fur Volkerkunde, Berlin; 19t WFA/British Museum; 19b AA/ Dagli Orti/Museo Del Templo Mayor, Mexico; 21 Corbis/ Jorge Gonzalez/EPA; 23 Dagli Orti/Museo del Templo Mayor; 25 akg-images/Bibliotheque Nationale, Paris; 26 WFA/National Museum of Anthropology; 29 Corbis/Dagli Orti; 30l AA/Eileen Tweedy/ British Museum; 30r AA/Dagli Orti/ National Anthropological Museum, Mexico; 32 Corbis/EPA/Ulises Ruiz; 35 AA/Dagli Orti /National Anthropological Museum; 36 AA/Dagli Orti/Museo del Templo Mayor, Mexico; 37 AA/Dagli Orti/National Anthropological Museum;

39 & 40t AA/Dagli Orti/Museo Cuidad Mexico; 40b WFA/N.J. Saunders; 41t akg-images; 41b BAL/Private collection; 43 WFA/ Bilblioteca Universitaria, Bologna; 44 Corbis/Gianni Dagli Orti; 46 BAL/Museo Degli Argenti, Palazzo Pitti, Florence; 47t&b Lord Price Collection; 49 AA; 50 BAL/Boltin Picture Library; 52 Getty Images/ National Geographic; 55 WFA/N.J. Saunders; 56-57 Corbis/Alison Wright; 58t WFA/David Bernstein, New York; 58b WFA/N.J. Saunders; 59t AA/Dagli Orti/Archaeological & Ethnological Museum, Guatemala City; 59b Corbis/Yann Arthus-Bertrand; 61 Corbis/Gianni Dagli Orti; 63l WFA/Edward H. Merrin Gallery, New York; 63r BAL/Private Collection; 64 WFA/Museum Fur Volkerkunde, Berlin; 65t Corbis/ Sygma; 65b Getty Images/Panoramic Images; 67 WFA/Private Collection, New York; 68–69 Corbis/Werner Forman; 70 Corbis/ Hans Georg Roth; 73 BAL/Museum of Fine Arts, Houston, Texas; 74 Corbis/Frans Lanting; 77 AA/Dagli Orti/Museo Del Polpol Vuh, Guatemala; 79 AA/Dagli Orti/Campeche Regional Museum; 80t BAL; 80b WFA/Museum Fur Volkerkunde,Berlin; 81t Corbis/Macduff Everton; 81b Corbis/Ludovic Maisant; 83 BAL/Museum of Fine Arts, Boston, Mass; 84 AA/Dagli Orti/Palenque Site Museum Chiapas; 86 AA/Dagli Orti/National Anthropological Museum, Mexico; 88 AA/Nicolas Sapieha